DOC SUSIE,
MY NEIGHBOR

DOC SUSIE,
MY NEIGHBOR

BY OWEN BRIGGS

•———•

Filter Press, LLC

ISBN: 978-0-86541-254-5
LCCN: 2018966884

Published by
Filter Press, LLC
Palmer Lake, Colorado

Manufactured in the United States of America

CONTENTS

Author Owen Briggs with his Aunt Hazel Briggs and Aunt Minnie Cole in 1954.

I feel uniquely qualified to add to the lore and information about the life of Doc Susie Anderson. She was my next-door neighbor for several years. Much of her life history has been written and rewritten numerous times in magazine articles, newspapers, and books, but I am one of the last persons alive to have known her personally and have memories of her as her neighbor.

This book shares my recollections from childhood and photographs from Doc's own albums and keepsakes, many of which have been in my care for decades. My Aunt Hazel was the executor of Doc's estate. Aunt Hazel had the monumental task of disposing of all of Doc's belongings and deciding what to save. Luckily, I have many of those items, photographed and first published here. I've let the images tell the tale and added narrative only as it explains or expands the story.

Because we were next-door neighbors, my family had a special relationship with one of the heroes of early medical care in Colorado. Doc Susie was among the first female physicians in Colorado. She was the only physician in Fraser, Colorado, for almost fifty years, treating both animals and humans. She was the first woman to be appointed county coroner in Colorado. In spite of suffering from tuberculosis, she lived a long life, long enough to experience the Cripple Creek Gold Rush and to treat skiers at Winter Park ski resort.

I refer to Dr. Susan Anderson throughout this book as 'Doc' because she was invariably called Doc by my family and all of Fraser.

INTRODUCTION

CHAPTER 01

DOC'S FAMILY

Doc's father was William H. Anderson. He was born in 1850, in Allen County, Indiana, and died in California in 1938. Doc Susie and her father did not always get along. However, she kept photographs and letters from him throughout the years.

William H. Anderson 1850-1938.

Doc saved this report card as a memento of her father.

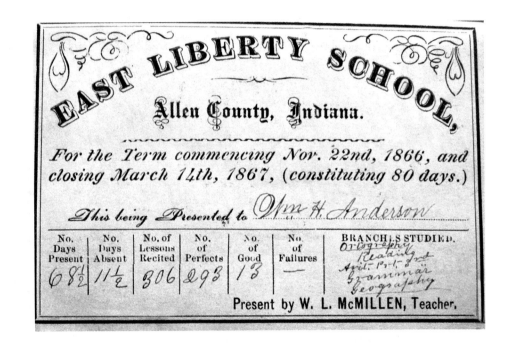

EAST LIBERTY SCHOOL,

Allen County, Indiana.

For the Term commencing Nov. 22nd, 1866, and closing March 14th, 1867, (constituting 80 days.)

This being Presented to *Wm H. Anderson*

No. Days Present	No. Days Absent	No. of Lessons Recited	No. of Perfects	No. of Good	No. of Failures	BRANCHES STUDIED.
68½	11½	306	293	13	—	Ortography Reading 1st Arit. Prt 1st 2nd Grammar Geography

Present by W. L. McMILLEN, Teacher.

This photo is thought to be John Anderson.

Doc's younger brother is on the right with unidentified companion.

Doc was very close to her brother John, who was two years younger than she. These photographs of John were in her personal collection.

DAVID ANDERSON   ABRAM ANDERSON   WILLIAM ANDERSON

These fine-looking gentlemen may have been Doc Susie's great uncles. The labels are as Doc wrote them on the reverse of the photograph, but the relationship to her is unknown. William Anderson was likely her paternal grandfather.

CHAPTER 02

YOUTH

Susan Anderson as a baby.

Susan Anderson was born January 31, 1870, in Nevada Mills, Indiana. Her father, William Anderson, was of Scotch-Irish descent. Doc described her mother, Marya, as "part Indian." There is no record of the date of their marriage, but they were divorced in 1875. Doc was 5 years old, and her brother John was 3.

Following the divorce, William took the two children (without Marya's consent), boarded a train, and ended up in Wichita, Kansas, where his parents had a homestead. He and the children lived with his parents, and he helped run the homestead.

The study of medicine ran in the family. Doc's great-grandfather and great-uncle were both country doctors, and her paternal grandmother was the neighborhood nurse. William wanted to be a doctor but had no opportunity for education and training. He did become a self-taught veterinarian. He wanted his son to become a doctor, but John had no interest in medicine. Doc's grandmother (who was also named Susan) taught her to crochet, cook, keep house, and have good manners. Doc really didn't care for all the domestic stuff. She wanted to do her own thing, and her own thing was to be an independent woman.

Susan Anderson, Doc's grandmother, for whom she was named.

Doc Susie graduated from high school in 1891 in Wichita, Kansas. From the commence program we learn that Doc's high school studies were centered on Latin and Greek in the Classical Course of studies. It would be interesting to know what she had to say about "Skilled and Unskilled Labor" in her senior essay.

Doc Susie - High School Graduation - 1891.

After high school, Doc learned Morse code and aspired to become a telegrapher, one of the few respectable occupations for women in the late 1800s. Life took Doc in a different direction, and she never worked as a telegrapher.

The telegraph machine Doc used to learn Morse code.

Doc's Half-siblings

Susie's mother, Marya (1848-1919), remarried in 1882 to a man named William McLaughlin. The couple had three children. Two are pictured here.

Left: Cuba and Louis McLaughlin with Marya. **Right:** Cuba and Marya.

Doc's father remarried in 1891 to Minnie Ethel Croy, a woman who was just a few years older than Doc. William and Minnie eventually had three children: a daughter (Cozette) and two sons (Vernon & Kenneth).

HATTIE COZETTE ANDERSON
Doc's half-sister

CARY HERMAN ANDERSON

The reverse of photograph identifies the children as Hattie Cozette Anderson and Cary Herman Anderson. Hattie was Doc's half-sister.

PHYSICIAN'S RECORD

PLACE OF BIRTH

County _El Paso. Teller._
Town of _Anaconda_
City of _Cripple Creek._
Street and No.
Name _Hattie Cozette Anderson._
Sex _Female_ Legitimate _Yes._
Twin, Triplet } _Single_ {No. in
or other } and {order of birth }
Father's Name _W.H. Anderson_
Color _White_ Age _4_
Birthplace _Monroeville Indiana_
Occupation _Miner_
Mother's } _Minnie Ethel Cray._
Maiden Name }
Color _White_ Age
Birthplace _Albert Lea Minnesota_
Occupation _Housewife_
Number of Child } _1_ { Number of Chil- } _1_
of this mother } { dren of this }
 { mother now living }
Date of Birth _Feb. 18 1896_ _P.M._

Courtesy Grand County Historical Association.

Doc kept the Physician's Birth Record of her half-sister, Hattie Cozette Anderson, born 1896. The certificate is part of the Doc Susie collection on display at the Grand County Pioneer Village Museum in Hot Sulphur Springs, Colorado.

In 1892, William sold his parents' homestead in Wichita and moved to Cripple Creek, Colorado, to join the gold rush in full swing there. John and Doc moved with him. They lived in this log cabin in Anaconda, a small town near Cripple Creek.

In the mid-1890s, the population in Cripple Creek was around 35,000 and included:

91 Lawyers   **80** Doctors   **14** Newspapers   **46** Brokerage houses

01 Coroner   **100** Saloons   **41** Assay Offices

Anaconda was a mining town of 2,000 people in 1904. The 1900 City Directory lists "Mrs." Susie Anderson and her father as living near the public school.

Anaconda Colo looking N E

Photos courtesy of Cripple Creek District Museum.

Doc with friends sometime in the 1890s. The photo is undated but appears to be from the Cripple Creek years. The third male figure from the left could be John Anderson, but the photo is unlabeled.

A year after the move to Colorado, Doc enrolled at the University of Michigan in Ann Arbor. She was 23 years old. Her brother also left Cripple Creek and went to college in Oakland, California, to study civil engineering. John mailed a postcard from Oakland instructing Susie on how to ship his guitar to him.

John's postcard transcribed.

Susie,

I forgot to tell you how to direct the box. Put my address on it. I am anxious about the guitar too. I wish you would have a kind of crate put around it and if that can't be done put it in its own box and have a light box put around it and sent it by express. You know the books are heavy and I am afraid of having it mashed. Excuse me for being so particular. I don't want to trouble you but I want the things all right when they get here. The weather is a little disagreeable today but may clear up as it generally does in the after noon. I haven't seen Ettiene yet. I sent for a paper the other day. It has some mining news in [it] I thought he might like to read. I am well. Good bye from John Anderson.

CHAPTER 03

MEDICAL SCHOOL

1893 - 1897

In 1893, Doc left Colorado to begin medical school at the University of Michigan. At that time, an undergraduate degree was not required to enter medical training.

The University of Michigan School of Medicine class of 1897 included 13 women among its 64 members.

Doc and fellow University of Michigan Medical School students. She is fourth from left in the fourth row. *Photo courtesy of Grand County Historical Association.*

PLEASE ADMIT

Miss Anderson

TO WARD TO STUDY CASE OF

Mrs Beaver

This hospital permission slip gave Doc permission to evaluate a patient.

Doc seated in center of a group of students in a U of Michigan classroom. *Photo courtesy of Grand County Historical Association.*

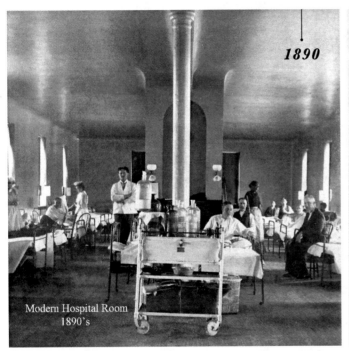

1890

Modern Hospital Room
1890's

A typical 1890s hospital ward.

1895

Doc and an unidentified friend, 1895.

In 1896, near the beginning of her third year in medical school, Doc's father withdrew all financial support. Doc did not know why. Her father gave no reason for not helping her, but she felt it was because she had searched for, and finally found, her biological mother. Doc had no contact with her mother for twenty years. Marya had remarried. She and her second husband and their three children were living in Ohio.

There was another likely reason that her father withdrew his support. Doc's stepmother resented the fact that William was providing money for Doc and John's schooling. She felt that the money should be used for their own family, which included three children.

During her junior year, another misfortune befell Doc. She contracted tuberculosis. She believed she got the disease while working night duty at Catherine Street Hospital, the University of Michigan's teaching hospital in Ann Arbor. This condition was very troubling for her and affected her everyday activities for years. Tuberculosis was one reason she returned to Colorado years later to be close to her father and brother. Her TB did not abate until she eventually moved to the colder, dryer climate of Fraser, Colorado.

Medical school tuition was a whopping $70.00 per year. To stay in school, Doc had to borrow money from her friend Mary Lapham. Much later, in the 1930s, Doc wrote to Mary offering to repay the loan. The reply letter from Mary states in the first sentence that the money was a gift, not a loan.

September 17, 1931

Dear Dr. Anderson,
I never loaned you any money. It was purely a good will offering to help you on your way—and I was glad to do it. I couldn't do it now for there have been heavy losses and so serious a reduction in income that it is all I can do to manage—a bad heart muscle has kept me a prisoner unable to do much of anything excepting play cards for the last five years. Physical efforts are beyond me—but I can have a good time sitting still and my friends take me driving so that I might be much worse off. It is nice to hear from you and to infer that you are getting along all right. That gives me a great deal of pleasure.
With kindest regards.
Sincerely
Mary Lapham

This student newspaper, dated October 2, 1897, is an example of items found in Doc's home after her death. The significance of this edition is unknown, and there may have been no direct significance. Doc seldom threw things away.

Dr. Susan Anderson's medical school graduation portrait, 1897.

Photo courtesy of Cripple Creek District Museum.

CHAPTER 04

CRIPPLE CREEK

In 1897 Doc moved back to Cripple Creek to start her practice. Her office was on the second floor of the Bimetallic Bank Building.

Doc was one of 55 physicians practicing in Cripple Creek. At first, she treated mostly women until she was able to save a boy's arm from amputation after he'd been told by other physicians that it should be amputated.

At this time, Cripple Creek's population was more than 30,000, which was remarkable considering much of the town had burned down the previous year.

1896

One year prior to Doc's return, the boomtown was nearly wiped out in April 1896 by two fires in one week.

The fire of 1896. *Photo courtesy of Cripple Creek District Museum.*

Bennett Avenue, Cripple Creek, in 1897 after rebuilding.

Bennett Avenue looking east in 1908. Note the trolley car. *Photo courtesy of Cripple Creek District Museum.*

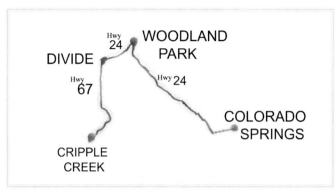

Today's roads from Colorado Springs to Cripple Creek take the driver through Woodland Park and Divide, approximately 45 miles.

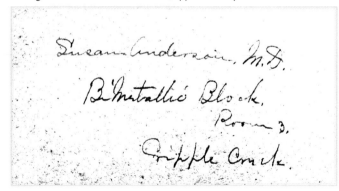

Doc's handwritten address from her grocery bill record book.

Street scene. Cripple Creek pre-1904. *Photo courtesy of Cripple Creek District Museum.*

Bennett Avenue in 2017 showing the Bimetallic Building on the far right. Doc's office was in the upstairs corner.

Doc was not without suitors during her years in Cripple Creek. In 1900, she was engaged to be married. The story goes that her father disliked the suitor and chased him away. Doc Susie herself never spoke of the suitor or the reason he left. Regardless of the reason, Doc was left at the altar, the marriage never took place, and her wedding dress, shown here, never worn.

The only known photograph of Doc and a boyfriend. The photo was found after her death among her papers.

Doc's wedding dress.

In 1900, Doc's brother John returned to Cripple Creek and shortly after became very ill with pneumonia. When she went to his side, Doc saw that he was beyond help. He died on March 16, 1900. It must have been very hard for Doc to know she had successfully seen so many others through pneumonia but was unable to save her brother.

After being left at the altar and her brother's death, Doc decided to move from Cripple Creek for a new start. At this time, she also was having problems in her relationship with her father and stepmother.

JOHN ANDERSON

Doc and her brother were very close. This photograph of John in his casket was among Doc's mementos found after her death.

CHAPTER 05

THE MOVE TO FRASER

Doc moved to Denver for a while, then to Steamboat Springs, and finally to Greeley, Colorado, where she worked as a nurse despite holding an MD degree.

While she was in Greeley, a diphtheria epidemic broke out. She had 300 patients in her care and was so overworked that her TB worsened. Doc was very frustrated that she was not allowed to work as a doctor. In those days, people would not go to a female doctor. According to Virginia Cornell, Doc Susie's biographer, one man in the area said he would rather be treated by his barber than a woman doctor.

FREIGHT BILL.

Form 748

8-05-200 M.
(Standard)

W H ANDERSON   DENVER COLO   Station, 2/21 1906.   190___

To UNION PACIFIC RAILROAD CO., Dr.

For Charges on Articles waybilled from   GREELEY COLO   via   U P

Pro. No.	5284	No. of Pkgs.	ARTICLES	WEIGHT	RATE	FREIGHT	ADVANCES
Date W.B.	2/19	1	COUCH				
W.B. No.	390	1	COUCH BACK			Notified by U.S. Mail. FEB 22 1906	
Whose Car	U P	1	CHAIR				
Car No.	65296	1	BOOK CASE BASE				
Consignor	S A	1	BOOK CASE TOP				
Shipping Point		10	BOXES HH GOODS				
		1	PICTURE WPD O R	1100	38	4. 18	
			REL VAL $5.00 CWT.				

BILL OF LADING SURRENDERED

RECEIVED PAYMENT FOR THE COMPANY,

UNION PACIFIC RAILROAD CO.
Local Freight Office.
___190__
FEB 24 1906

Claims for Overcharge and Loss or Damage must be sent to the Freight Claim Agent, Omaha, Nebraska, through this Company's local agent or representative at the point where claim originates, with this Freight Bill and the Original Bill of Lading attached.

Agent.
Per J. F. BARRON, AGT,
Per ___   Cashier.   TOTAL COLLECTED BY AGENT ___

GOODS MUST BE REMOVED WITHIN TWENTY-FOUR HOURS AFTER ARRIVAL.

Doc's household goods, consisting of 1,100 pounds, were shipped in 1906 from Greeley, Colorado. The cost of $4.18 appears to have been paid by her father.

Doc stored her household items for one month in 1907. The charge was $2.00. The swastika symbol used in the logo of the transfer company was borrowed from Native American art and folklore.

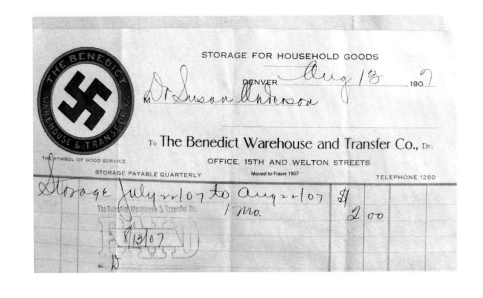

STORAGE FOR HOUSEHOLD GOODS

DENVER, Aug 13 190

M Dr Susan Anderson

To The Benedict Warehouse and Transfer Co., Dr.

OFFICE, 15TH AND WELTON STREETS

STORAGE PAYABLE QUARTERLY   Moved to Fraser 1907   TELEPHONE 1260

Storage July 22/07 to Aug 22/07 $ 2 00
1 mo.

THE BENEDICT WAREHOUSE & TRANSFER CO.

THE SYMBOL OF GOOD SERVICE

PAID 8/13/07

1907

To try to heal her tuberculosis, in August 1907, Doc decided to move with her little white Spitz dog to Fraser, Colorado, to either be cured or die. She would have known the odds—one in every four tuberculosis victims did not recover from the disease.

At that time there were only twelve houses in Fraser. The town had about the same number of saloons and an opera house. The temperature often dipped to 60 below zero. Over time, she was cured of the disease.

Her first home in Fraser was a little shack by the railroad tracks. Virginia Cornell's book recounts how she established her reputation as a doctor: One night a cowboy knocked on Doc's front door. He was all excited and told Doc that she had to come with him right away because, "Davey is hurt and needs help right now." Doc grabbed her medical bag and off they went. When they arrived at the scene of the accident, she found that Davey was a horse. Davey had gotten tangled up with a barbed wire fence and had some very bad cuts. Doc took care of the wounds, Davey recovered and had no subsequent problems due to the injuries. In fact, Doc did such a good job mending Davey that she was now recognized as a very competent medical doctor by Fraser's citizens, and in time, the whole of Grand County.

An unknown figure stands in the doorway of Doc Susie's first office in Fraser.

1914 - 1918

A few years after she arrived in Fraser, World War I started in 1914 and lasted until 1918. Doc's life was not disrupted by the war, but on the heels of the Great War came the 1918 influenza epidemic. It killed more people than had died in the war. Mortality in Colorado from influenza was the fifth highest in the nation, and Fraser had its share of deaths, many attended by Doc.

Doc was often seen around Fraser. Here she is photographed, in bonnet, with a friend in front of the Fraser Opera House in 1917.

Courtesy of Grand County Historical Association

Fraser as Doc would have known it.

Fraser was founded in February 1874 and was named after Reuben Frazer, a pioneer settler. The town is in Grand County, which is also the headwaters of the Colorado River. The elevation is 8,574 feet above sea level.

Fraser, Colorado, looking west from Highway 40, 1920s.

1920

Fraser, Colo. 1920's

A Fraser street looking east in 1920s.

1928

Bl6 Fraser, Colorado. 1928

Fraser, 1928, looking west.

The town looking South. The undated photograph is labeled, "Fraser, Colo. At foot of Berthoud Pass."

44

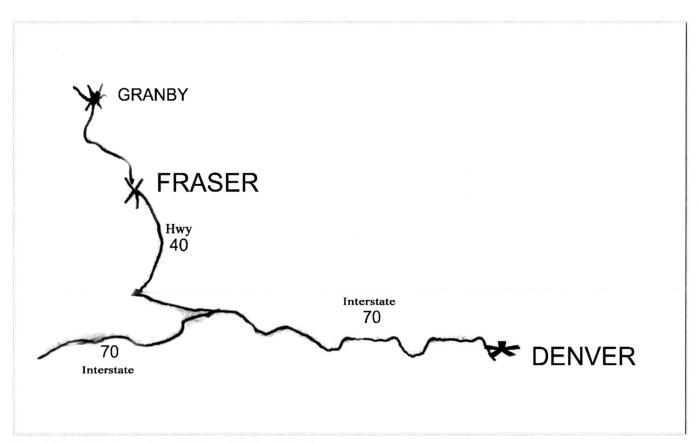

Fraser is located 73 miles northwest of Denver via I-70 and US 40.

LIFE IN FRASER

Receipts and letters give some insights into Doc's life as a country doctor and town resident. She ordered fruit and medical supplies from Denver, paid her taxes, received invitations to marry and invitations to visit friends, bought property, and befriended her neighbors, including eventually an 8-year-old boy named Owen Briggs.

U. S. Department of Agriculture,

FOREST SERVICE.

FREE-USE PERMIT.

......Arapaho...... **National Forest,**

................September 1,—, 1900

I hereby apply for permission to take,

within ....6.... *months from* .Sept 1,

Mar 1,......., 1900, *from* .W 1/2 of

NW 1/4 sec 14, T 2 S, R 75 W.

6th P.M.
_(Describe lands.)

the following-described timber: .Dead...
_{(Specify species}

.Lodgepole pine and Engelmann
_{and state whether dead or living ; number of cords and value per cord;}

.Spruce timber for fire-wood..
_{number of feet B. M. and value per thousand; number and dimensions of}

.10 cords at $25 per cord....
_{house logs, posts, or other special products; and rate of valuation.)}

worth .$.2.50......; *to be used by me*

.at my residence in Fraser,......
_(How and where.)

.Colo.

c8—426   (OVER.)

Name — *Value* — *Dollars* — *Cts.*

In consideration of such permission I
agree to—

1. Cut only such timber as is designated by a Forest officer.

2. Remove no timber until permission is given.

3. Conduct the cutting and dispose of the refuse as directed by the Forest officer.

4. Neither sell, give away, or exchange any material taken.

5. Assist Forest officers to fight fire during the period of this permit.

6. Comply with all other regulations governing National Forests.

7. Comply with Sections 3739 to 3742, inclusive, Revised Statutes U. S.

Signed in duplicate this ....8.... *day*

of .September......................., 1900

Susan Anderson

................Fraser,..Colorado.
_(P. O. address.)

Approved, and permit granted under above
conditions.

J. S. Linscott

8—426

................Forest Ranger.
_(Title.)

This receipt from the U.S. Forest Service is for 10 cords of wood at 25 cents per cord for a grand total of $2.50. Doc, and everyone who was granted permission to cut wood in the National Forest, agreed to a list of conditions (on right).

1912

Doc often ordered medical supplies from Denver. This receipt from 1912 shows she paid 14 cents for two balls of cotton. Notice that one cent in change was returned to her.

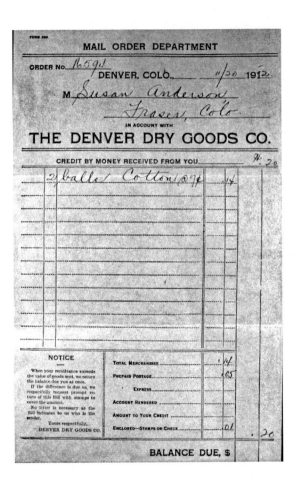

1913 - 1914

Doc's first property deed in 1913 was for the property next door to my Aunt Hazel and Uncle Bud. With ownership came taxes. Doc's first property tax bill was for $2.40 in 1914.

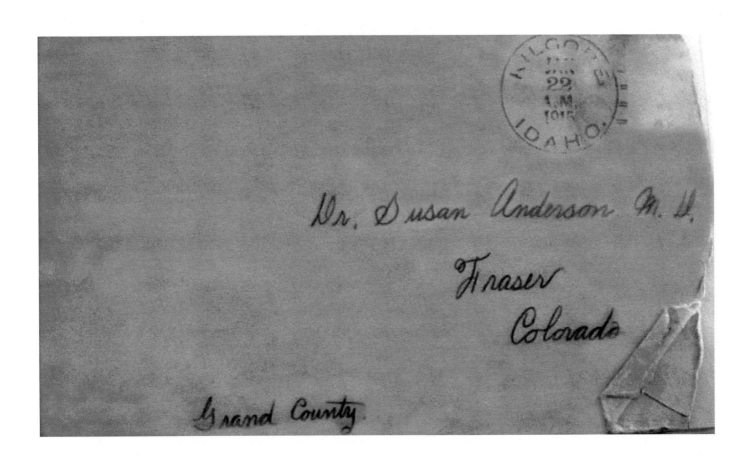

1915

In 1915, a letter came addressed to Dr. Susan Anderson M.D. from a boyfriend, or someone who considered himself her boyfriend. The letter offers reconciliation but raises more questions than answers. It was mailed on January 22, 1915, from Kilgore, Idaho, fifteen years after Doc had been left at the altar, so it is unlikely it is the same suitor. She kept the letter for the rest of her life, but there is no record that she ever replied.

Dubois Idaho 1-23-15

Dear Friend (if I may call you)

No doubt you will be more than surprised to hear from me as no doubt you must think I have forgotten you but such is not the case I often think of you and of how kind you were to me and wonder if I will ever see you again.

Now I do not know if you consider me worthy of an answer to this or not but at any rate I thought it my duty to at least write and let you know I am still alive.

I am just in receipt of a letter from my sister stating my mother is on her death bed and I expect any time to receive news of her death.

2

Ella also told me in her letter that she received an inquiry from you as to my whereabouts but owing to my previous trouble I have warned her against sending my address to people unknown to her to avoid all possible chance of further trouble. Of course you cannot blame me for that and I would not want you to feel hard against her for not advising you where I was and at any rate she did not know herself until Xmas.

Mrs Scott also wrote to Canada wanting to know where I was and made all kinds of threats to prosecute me if she could locate me. Ha! Ha! Ha! I wonder if she

3

thought sister would answer that. I sent her [Mrs Scott.] that letter you read and many others just as bad also various post cards with very plain facts written on them.

I have often felt very sorry for the harm I did Dorcas but I do not know as I am all to blame at any rate I offered to make amends and I guess the old woman has often wished she would have allowed it but I am very thankful now that she did not for I will tell you the truth that I never loved her or any one as I did you and as I still do you.

52

Now I am going to tell you the reason
I claimed to you to be married was
because I did not want you to be disgrace
by marrying an ex convict and I knew you
must surely find it out sometime if we
were married

I know I could always have been
happy with you but I feared your happiness
when the time would come for you to
find out the truth of the matter and
then in case there would have been another
in our family when you found it out it
would make it hard for you to leave
me without a father for the little one.

Now perhaps you think I did you wrong

but I did what I thought at that time
to be best for your own good.

I have not taken a drink since I left
Colorado and I have got two good teams
of horses and am working them every
day.

Now Dear as you know all about my
other life I am going to ask you if you
think you could be happy with me if
we were to get married and I was to
promise (and keep my promise) to do better
in the future and be the man and
husband that you would have me be.
Would you like to come out here in the
spring if I make every thing ready and

would you care to leave Colo.

I suppose there are some great changes
around there since I left.

I heard Dorcas eloped with some stranger
and that the old lady was quite mad
about it perhaps she would rather have
had her elope with me.

I wrote to every one that knew the
Scott family and told them all about
it.

Who took care of Dorcas when she
knocked the kid and was she pretty
sick.

I guess by her being so anxious to
get married that I must have given

her a taste of something she liked and
thought she must have.

Now if you think I am worthy of
an answer please write and tell me all
the news and give me your opinion
on coming out here with me.

Now I trust you will not let any
one know where I am as you know
it might mean serious trouble for one.

All for this time by hoping to hear
from you soon and by asking to be
allowed to remain As Ever & Always
Your True & Ever Loving Claude.

Address   W. M. Bennett
(Sealed with A. Kiss)   Dubois Idaho.

Dear Friend (if I may call you),

No doubt you will be more than surprised to hear from me as no doubt you must think I have forgotten you but such is not the case. I often think of you and of how kind you were to me and wonder if I will ever see you again.

Now I do not know if you consider me worthy of an answer to this or not but at any rate I thought it my duty to at least write and let you know I am still alive.

I am just in receipt of a letter from my sister stating my mother is on her death bed and I expect anytime to receive news of her death.

Ella also told me in her letter that she received an inquiry from you as to my whereabouts but owing to my previous trouble I have warned her against sending my address to people unknown to her to avoid all possible chance of further trouble.

Of course you cannot blame me for that and I would not want you to feel hard against her for not advising you where I was and at any rate she did not know herself until Xmas.

Mrs. Scott also wrote to Canada wanting to know where I was and made all kinds of threats to prosecute me if she could locate me. Ha! Ha! Ha! I wonder if she thought sister would answer that? I sent her (Mrs. Scott) that letter you read and many others just as bad also various post cards with very plain facts written on them.

I have often felt very sorry for the harm I did Dorcas but I do not know as I am all to blame at any rate I offered to make amends and I guess the old woman has often wished she would have allowed it but I am very thankful now that she did not for I will tell you the truth that I never Loved her or any one as I did you and as I still do you.

Now I am going to tell you the reason I claimed to you to be married was because I did not want you to be disgrace by marrying an ex convict and I knew you must surely find it out sometime if we were married.

I know I could always have been happy with you but I feared your happiness when the time would come for you to find out the truth of the matter and then in case there would have been another in our family when you found it out it would make it hard for you to leave me without a father for the little one.

Now perhaps you think I did you wrong but I did what I thought at that time to be best for your own good.

I have not taken a drink since I left Colorado and I have got two good teams of horses and am working them every day.

Now Dear as you know all about my other life I am going to ask you if you think you could be happy with me if we were to get married and I was to promise (and keep my promise) to do better in the future and be the man and husband that you would have me be. Would you like to come out here in the spring if I make ever thing ready and would you care to leave Colo.

I suppose there are some great changes around there since I left.

I heard Dorcas eloped with some stranger and that the old lady was quite mad about it perhaps she would rather have had her elope with me.

I wrote to every one that knew the Scott family and told them all about it.

Who took care of Dorcas when she knocked the kid and was she pretty sick.

I guess by her being so anxious to get married that I must have given her a taste of something she liked and thought she must have.

Now if you think I am worthy of an answer please write and tell me all the news and give me your opinion on coming out here with me.

Now I trust you will not let any one know where I am as you know it might mean serious trouble for me.

All for this time by hoping to hear from you soon and by asking to be allowed to remain As Ever & Always Your True & Ever Loving Claude

Address W. M. Bennett
Dubois, Idaho
(Sealed With A. Kiss.)

A shipment of 75 pounds of fruit from Denver to Fraser cost $ .64 in 1914.

THE ADY & CROWE MERCANTILE CO.

HAY AND GRAIN.

DENVER COLO.

Sold to   Susan Anderson,   10/6/17

CAR NO.   Fraser, Colo.

1 Sax Hen Feed   100#   3.90   3.90

We are out of wheat

Our responsibility ceases upon our obtaining from Railroad receipt for goods in good order. Claim for damage must be made to them.

1917

Doc kept chickens, as did most people in Fraser. The cost of chicken feed was $3.90 per 100 pounds. One hundred years later, in 2017, 100 pounds of chicken feed cost $30.

One of Doc's proposals of marriage came from the County Jail in Denver.

Dear Friend

Thought if you wanted a fine husband that there is sure one here in Denver when I come in and he soon will be coming out there when he comes back from fortlogan Colo. 24thCoBand. and this is his adress so you can wright out there to that adress. and when he gets acquainted with you he will be right out and will take you any place you want to go. so good by from Jess. S. Bashore.

His name is Harry A. Clark
His age is 26 years old.

and he has Ben in the Navy 3 years to and he is in the army now and if he finds awomen what he likes he will marry her. if she likes him so he is auffell good looking to and a soldier in U.S. Armey. and is amuscion to and can play the Clarnet. and hant going with no other girl now.

1917

On May 18, 1917, this notice was printed in the *Middle Park Times* newspaper:

> On account of indifferent health, I shall discontinue the practice of medicine for one year. Will my patients please make a note of the fact, and those knowing themselves indebted to me, kindly settle their accounts. Susan Anderson, M.D. Fraser, Colorado.

Doc had not been in Fraser long when the notice was printed. Where did she go? Did she stay away a year as she intended? What was the nature of her 'indifferent health'? These questions remain unanswered.

Invitations from friends to visit Sulfur Springs and Matheson, Colorado, 1919 and 1921.

Doc's father moved to California in 1900. In 1920, he sent a telegraph encouraging her to move to California and begin a medical practice there. She had no interest in moving.

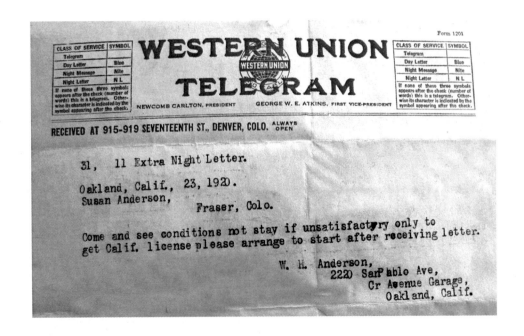

Doc's little white spitz dog was named Pooch. Pooch lived to be about 13 years old and died of cancer in 1920. Doc had him stuffed and kept him in her house for a few years.

Pooch looked a lot like the dog in the photograph.

1919 Warranty Deed for Doc's two lots in Fraser, Colorado.

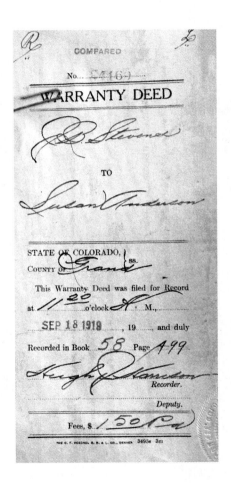

Form 171A—Revised 1903. WARRANTY DEED. For Sale by The C.P. Special Blank Book & Litho. Co. Denver, Colo. 34024

This Deed, Made this   First   day of Sept

in the year of our Lord one thousand nine hundred and Nineteen,

BETWEEN   J. B. Stevens,

of the   County of   Grand   and State of Colorado, of the first part, and

Susan Anderson,

of the County of   Grand   and State of Colorado, of the second part:

WITNESSETH, That the said party of the first part, for and in consideration of the sum of

One   Dollars,

to the said party of the first part in hand paid by the said party of the second part, the receipt

whereof is hereby confessed and acknowledged, has   granted, bargained, sold and conveyed, and by these

presents do   grant, bargain, sell, convey and confirm unto the said party of the second part,

her   heirs and assigns forever, all the following described lots   or parcel of land, situate,

lying and being in the County of   Grand   and State of Colorado, to-wit:

Lots 34-35 Blk 2   Town of Easton,

Know All Men by these Presents: March 16   1920

That in consideration of   One Dollar + other valuable DOLLARS,
services

the receipt of which is hereby acknowledged,   We   hereby sell and deliver unto   Dr

Susan Anderson   the following described   Log house   branded as follows:

One Log house 27 ft × 39 ft same to

be Removed from our Premises at once

And said grantor hereby covenants that he is the lawful owner of the above described property, that
the same is free and clear from incumbrances, and that he has good right to sell and dispose of same.

Stevens Bar T + L Co

By R M Robbins Asst Tre

FORM 6 1-2   THE W. H. KISTLER STATIONERY CO., DENVER

1920

Receipt and description of Doc's log house that she purchased for $1.00 from the rancher who at the time was using it as a barn. It was sold on the condition it be moved at once. The rancher charged Doc one dollar to make the transaction legal and make it clear it was not a gift. The barn made a fine house. In 2018, it was still standing and occupied.

The log house Doc bought for one dollar had to be moved immediately. Doc kept a list of friends and neighbors who helped and what she paid each to move the house and reassemble it on her two lots. I personally knew some of the people on the list.

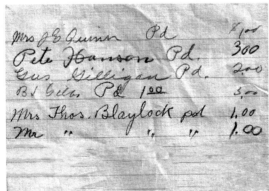

As the log house was disassembled to be moved, Doc marked each log by driving nails in the end of logs in numerical sequence. Many of the workers, who moved the house and reassembled it, did not speak English. By counting the nails, they were able to place the logs in the same order and put the house back together.

Doc had a telephone in her first office, which was down by the railroad tracks. She did not have a phone in her new house because she didn't like to use phones, and she couldn't afford to pay a phone bill.

Doc's log house.

Doc's log house is on the left. The two tall houses belonged to Uncle Bud.

Doc's roof piled with snow during a long Fraser winter.

Doc's friend Sam Evans in front of her log home.

Another snowy Fraser winter.

Uncle Bud's & Aunt Hazel's house is in the foreground on left and
Aunt Minnie's house is on the right. Doc's house (not shown) was
to the right of the two little houses.

1943

The big house that my Grandfather (Manfred Clyde Briggs) and I used as a bunkhouse.

Grandfather Briggs and me at home around 1943.

There were no laundry facilities in Fraser. Aunt Hazel did much of Doc's washing and ironing in summer and winter by hand using a washboard and tub. She ironed clothes with sadirons (the one pictured below belonged to Doc). Sadirons were heated on top of a stove. Ironing with them was tricky and time consuming.

Doc had no electricity in her log home. She used kerosene lamps (the lamp pictured above is one of hers). Her well was inside the house. The outhouse was back of the house by the alley. She used a wood burning stove to heat her house. In later years, she used propane to heat her home.

The University of Michigan requested information for
the annual Catalogue of Alumni and Former Students
of the University, and Doc complied.

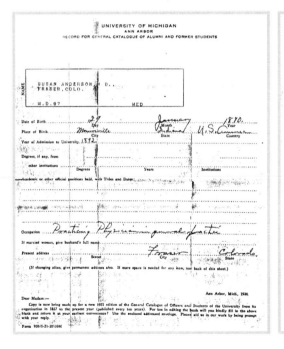

Doc kept in contact with the university. This 1929 letter is the reply she received after sending an inquiry and sample for evaluation to the Department of Chemistry. It would be interesting to know why she suspected something amiss in the sample sent. Note the interesting comment in the P. S. at the end of letter.

After 5 days, return to
DEPARTMENT OF CHEMISTRY,
University of Michigan,
ANN ARBOR, MICHIGAN

Dr. Susan Anderson

Fraser

Colorado

UNIVERSITY OF MICHIGAN
ANN ARBOR
DEPARTMENT OF CHEMISTRY

June 18, 1929

Dr. Susan Anderson
Fraser, Colo.

My dear Dr. Anderson:

I have examined the crystals in the package received from you and find that they are pure cane sugar. Just how it got into the glycerine or whether it was formed by some slow chemical reaction over a period of years is impossible to say. It is very rare, of course, to find crystallized glycerine; in fact we have had only one specimen in this laboratory for many years and that has long since disappeared. The melting point of pure glycerine crystals is around room temperature; consequently had it been glycerine it would have melted before reaching us, owing to the recent unusually warm weather here.

We appreciate very much your interest in taking care that this University should be the one to receive the specimen. It is quite evident that you are a loyal alumnus.

Sincerely yours,

H. H. Willard

Prof., Analytical Chemistry

HHWillard/m

P. S. During the war glycerine was so scarce that much of it was diluted with syrup (to maintain viscosity) and this may have been such a sample.

76

An unknown photographer captured Doc picking berries in the early 1920s in the Fraser Valley.

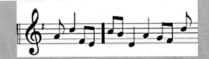

Doc liked to sing and loved the songs "Oh, What a Beautiful Morning" and "Mockingbird Hill." Many times, she would sing some of the words to one or the other when she was in a happy mood.

She liked to recite her favorite poems, "Grandmother" and "My Bible," and did so often. During conversations with friends or patients, she frequently quoted a verse or a passage from the Bible.

My Bible

The book my grandmother gave me,
As I sat by her gracious knee,
My dear little, fat, black Bible!
It is all the world to me.

How I love those wonderful stories
Of Moses and John and Paul,
Of how David killed the giant,
And Samuel heard the call.

How Daniel dared the lions,
And the angry jaws grew still,
How Jericho's walls were shaken,
By the Lord's own mighty will.

Best of all, how the Master
Walked the shores of Galilee,
Healing the sick and the sinner,
And stilling the tossing sea.

For the Word of God is mighty,
And the arm of the Lord is strong,
To hold back the powers of darkness,
And keep His child from wrong.

Oh, the beauty of the Bible
And its glories never cease!
They fill my soul with wonder,
And the angels' song of peace.

(Published in *The American Standard*, October 15, 1925)

Grandmother

Author unknown

Grandmother on a winter's day
Milked the cows and fed them hay,
Slopped the hogs, saddled the mule,
And got the children off to school.
Did a washing, mopped the floors,
Washed the windows, and did some chores.
Cooked a dish of home-dried fruit,
Pressed her husband's Sunday suit,
Swept the parlor, made the bed
Baked a dozen loaves of bread;
Split some firewood and lugged in
Enough to fill the kitchen bin.
Cleaned the lamps and put in oil,
Stewed some apples she thought would spoil.

Churned the butter, baked the cake
Then exclaimed, "For Heaven's sake, the
calves have got out of the pen!"
Went and chased them in again.
Gathered eggs and locked the stable,
Back to the house and set the table.
Cooked a supper that was delicious
And afterwards washed all the dishes.
Fed the cat and sprinkled the clothes,
Mended a basketful of hose,
Then opened the organ and began to play:
***"When you come to the end of a
perfect day."***

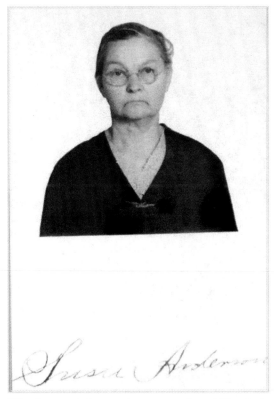

This photograph is a good representation of Doc Susie as a middle-aged woman. Neither the exact date nor the occasion of this photograph is known.

During Prohibition, Doc was deputized to assist law enforcement in uncovering hidden stills and alcohol. She took her role seriously. Once, she uncovered six pints of hooch (whiskey) from a Fraser resident. That person spent 30 days in jail and paid a $300.00 fine. [Recounted in *The Magnificent Mountain Women* by Janet Robertson]

The writer seems to refer to a baby delivered by Doc under trying circumstances.

Topeka, Kas 10.20.1922

Dear Miss Anderson—
You will think it queer to hear from me but queer things happen, don't they? I am applying for a job with the Santa Fe Ry. And they want references as to my work in 1917, 18, 19 and 20, or that is more in particular they want to know I wasn't making moonshine, or running a gambling house, or something. I have referred them to you.

I was in the crate business with a mill of my own all the last two years near Salida, but the head lettuce business hurt that whole country and put us out of business so I am going back to the railroad telegraphing and newspaper work. The boys are all busy in school at Salida. Channing is developing wonderfully in music, when we make our stake we will come out there and make a permanent home somewhere. Gertrude has been so well & strong since Lincoln's birth—that I will never forget our trip that night!—I hope this finds you well and happy. As ever,
E.A. Van Camp

In 1923, Doc was hired as the official railroad doctor for Grand County.

A work train as it comes through Fraser, Colorado.

This train is typical of the passenger and mail trains that rumbled through Fraser twice daily.

This letter was sent from Tabernash, Colorado, a town four miles north of Fraser. [Interesting that the note is dated January 21 and yet it closes by wishing Doc a Merry Christmas.]

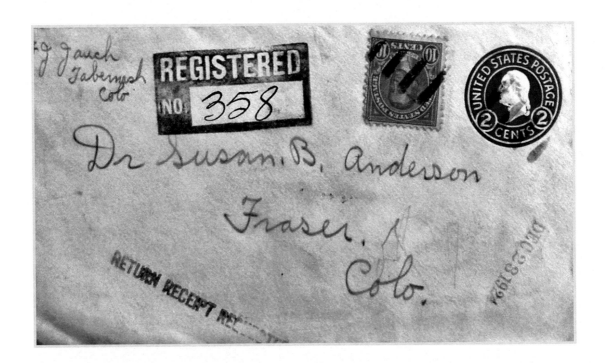

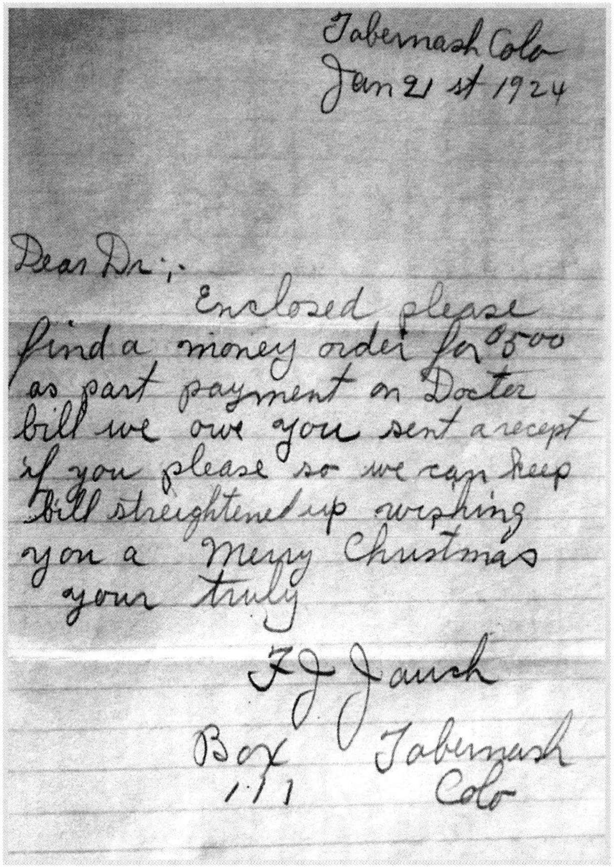

Tabernash Colo
Jan 21 st 1924

Dear Dr;:

Enclosed please find a money order for 5⁰⁰ as part payment on Docter bill we owe you sent a recept if you please so we can keep bill streightened up wishing you a Merry Christmas
your truly

F J Janch
Box 111 Tabernash Colo

Tabernash Colo
Jan 21st 1924

Dear Dr.,

Enclosed please find a money order for \$5.00 as part payment on Doctor bill we owe you sent a recept if you please so we can keep bill steightened up wishing you a Merry Christmas.

Your truly

FJ Janck
Box 111   Tabenash Colo

Doc saved the front page of the *Santa Ana Register* reporting the stock market crash and the onset of the Great Depression. It's likely that the California newspaper was mailed to her by her father.

1926 - 1933

Doc was appointed the county coroner of Grand County in 1926. She served in that position for one year and again in 1930 and 1931. After testifying at a court trial in which two men were found guilty and were sent to the gallows, she decided that she didn't care for that kind of work.

In 1932, Doc became homesick and wanted to move back to her childhood home in Indiana. She packed her belongings and shipped it all to Indiana. She had plans to have flowerbeds with roses as roses were her favorite flower. By April 1933, she found that the Indiana that she remembered just wasn't there anymore. The people were not the same, and she felt that she was not going to be accepted as she thought she would be. She moved her belongings

back to good old Fraser, Colorado. The whole town welcomed her back with open arms. Below is the copy of the freight bill from Angola, Indiana, to Fraser (spelled *Frazier* by the carrier).

Even though times were tough and patients did not always pay their bills, Doc was able to save some money in a savings account at Colorado National Bank. Doc opened her account March 23, 1931, with a balance of $133.80. She closed her account on December 22, 1954, with a balance of $1,821.14.

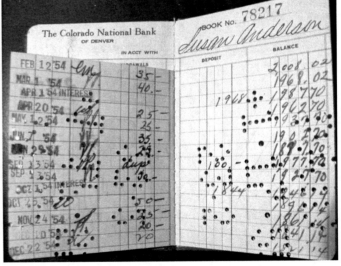

Doc Susie bought her groceries on credit. This record book is for her account with Mr. O'Loughlin, a grocer in Fraser. She used it to log in all her purchases. She wrote the name of the item, date of purchase, and the cost. She totaled all entries monthly and paid the grocer. Incidentally, she never bought meat because she had no refrigeration.

CHAPTER 07

FRASER'S PHYSICIAN

An undated photo of Doc likely made in the late 1920s or early 1930s.

SUSAN ANDERSON, M. D.
FRASER, COLORADO

A sample of Doc's letterhead

Doc Susie at Fraser Depot with her medical bag (1930s).

Kids in town took their sick or injured pets to Doc Susie for treatment. They knew Doc would take care of them.

Once, when Aunt Hazel's dog injured a paw, it went straight to Doc's house next door for help.

1950

Uncle Bud Briggs' team of horses and his bobsled were often Doc's transportation to patients, especially during winter. Once during a snowstorm, Doc was needed about 30 miles away. The train was held for her and Uncle Bud drove Doc four miles to Tabernash with his team and sled to catch the train. Neither Uncle Bud nor Doc were intimidated by a snowstorm. This incident was written about in the book *Rails That Climb* by Edward Bollinger, originally published in 1950.

My Uncle Bud with the team of horses he used to make sure Doc got to her patients.

Uncle Bud in the background was preparing to transport Doc to an emergency call using his bobsled and team of horses. Doc never owned a car. In winter she frequently relied on Uncle Bud for help since he was right next door.

She dressed warmly in winter using layers of clothes, including long underwear, high boots, mittens, and a wool scarf.

Doc was our family physician as well as our neighbor. While working as a lumberjack, Uncle Bud was cutting logs and trimming branches with an axe. He swung the axe to cut a branch, but it glanced in a different direction and cut his leg very badly. A coworker applied a tourniquet and took him to Doc. She stopped the bleeding and stitched up the wound, of course, without pain killers or sedatives. She never used them for any situation.

Another time, Doc diagnosed a skin problem on Uncle Bud's face as melanoma and cautioned him to have it removed as soon as possible. My grandmother came from Laramie, Wyoming, and transported him to Mayo Brothers Cancer Center in Minnesota where surgery was performed. The cancer surgeon told Uncle Bud that this type of cancer was very aggressive, that Doc Susie correctly identified the problem, and had recommended the correct treatment.

Aunt Hazel in front of Doc's house.

Aunt Hazel occasionally needed to split wood for our wood burning stove. One evening she was splitting some kindling to be used the next morning to cook breakfast. As she was swinging the axe to split the wood, her middle finger on her left hand got in the way and was cut off at the middle joint. Aunt Hazel picked up her finger and ran over to Doc Susie's house/office. Doc cleaned and stitched the wound. She put Aunt Hazel's finger in a bottle of alcohol, and Aunt Hazel kept it for a few years.

When I was about eight years old, I accidently stepped on a rusty nail that was sticking out of the frozen ground. Doc treated it using a swab dipped in alcohol to clean the wound. After cleaning it three or four times she bandaged it. I was on crutches for two weeks, and the wound healed perfectly. As usual, when treating a patient for whatever might be wrong, she used no pain killers whatsoever.

I am eight years old in this photo taken behind Uncle Bud and Aunt Hazel's house. Doc's log house is behind me.

Around the same time, Doc and I were photographed together. I'm not sure I was meant to be in the photograph!

1951

One day in 1951 Uncle Bud was riding one of his horses when the horse slipped on some ice, fell, and landed on its side with my Uncle's leg pinned between the horse and frozen ground. The accident broke Uncle Bud's leg in two places. He struggled and finally was able to get back on the horse and made it to Doc Susie's home and office. She splinted his leg and furnished crutches. The leg soon mended.

Doc sometimes helped supervised me. Uncle Bud always told me, "Do not go on the other side of the railroad tracks because of safety reasons." Well, one day while Uncle Bud was still on crutches from the horse falling on him, I did cross the tracks to play with my friends. I thought that he would never come after me, especially while he was on crutches. I was wrong, he did find me, and I was disciplined.

I found out later that Doc Susie saw me playing where I was not supposed to be, and she made sure that Uncle Bud knew all about it.

Doc treated my Grandfather Briggs and diagnosed a hernia. She sent him to University of Denver for surgery. This is the cover letter and report she received concerning grandfather's case.

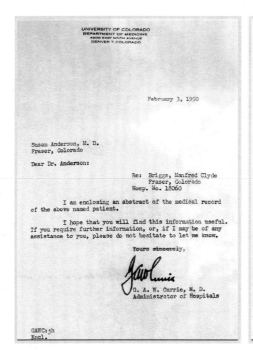

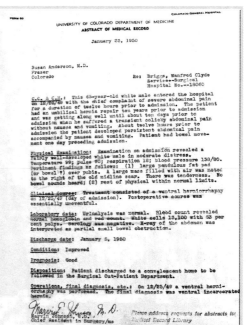

Doc Susie—Our Neighbor

Doc was a petite lady. She was 5-feet, 1-inch tall and weighed around 100 pounds when she came to Fraser. Her hair was always up in a bun. She wore glasses, was very pleasant to talk to, and always friendly.

Doc came to our house every morning, right after Uncle Bud milked our Jersey cow named Bossy. She always had a glass of body-warm milk for breakfast. She ate meals at our house quite often, and she always scolded me for using too much pepper. "It's not good for your liver," Doc would tell me. Doc herself always drank coffee with lemon juice. She said it was good for headaches and other ailments.

In the winter Doc would come to our house about two hours before going to bed. She always brought a large sadiron with her. Aunt Hazel would put the iron in the wood burning stove oven and heat it up. When it got hot enough she wrapped it in two or three layers of newspaper, then a heavy cloth, so it would stay as hot as possible. Doc took the hot iron home and put it under the covers at the foot of her bed to keep her feet warm during the night. Aunt Hazel walked her home at night using a flashlight. There were no street lights or electric lights.

Doc was not exempt from pranks and jokes. One Halloween night while she was sleeping, a bunch of kids tipped over her outhouse. The next morning one of our horses got loose and accidently fell in the open toilet hole. It took three people about six hours to get him out and another hour just to wash him off. Uncle Bud and I set the toilet back up and all was ok.

Doc standing in front of her log home. Entrance to her medical office is behind her left shoulder. Inside her office was a metal exam table, her desk, and clutter everywhere. The entrance hallway was just wide enough to walk through cautiously because boxes were piled on top of each other on both sides all the way to the ceiling.

In 1938, the year of his death, Doc wrote to her father for the last time.

Fraser Colo.
Jan 13. 1938.

Pa: It is so strange to me that I write you something I expect fully to hear from and wait + wait for an answer and wonder what has happened to keep you from writing. then finally you write and wonder why you dont hear from me, I certainly do wish it could be possible for me to do something to take you out of the home. a home of my own in some pleasant country. But it seems next to impossible I certainly can not think of selling my home here + putting the proceeds into hunting for gold as is too uncertain. this is the only shelter I have in the world and here is the only chance for income beside manual labor somewhere else and I am too old to go out to hard work for others. this month will make the end of 68 years for me too old to earn my keep by hard labor. I never did want to go to California to live, and nothing ever will make it attractive to me. Just now I dont care to go to the west coast on account of the possibility of war with Japan.

You will just simply divide any thing I say in that direction so I might just as well not say it. I know how you think about California and, no amount of argument will change you, but it doesnt appeal to me in any way whatever.
If I could get something in Indiana it would be home to me. I have met a lot of people from Missouri and Arkansas and think more of that country than California but it is not possible for me to get any thing. And as for selling my house you cant do it. There is no sale for any thing even good property in Denver will have to sell away down from the cost of building. I would be almost penniless for me to get rid of this. You can hunt gold without me giving up my only refuge. California was not such a pleasant place last winter and this winter isnt over yet. Yesterday was a stormy one here but not very cold the wind blew. it snowed but not extremely low temperature. I am willing for you to hunt for gold, if you dont put yourself in a helpless position as you did last time and then send for help to get out of the hole. I am not making any money but just living. What I'd made last summer must last me till spring because there is no one here working now and it is almost impossible to collect back bills. Every body hangs on to money as hard as you ever saw. Just to have enough

to get on till Spring. There is no let up
of hard times yet. Nothing in sight to
make good times and a prospect of war.
I'm sorry if Kenneth is sick and there
is no way I can help him because he
wouldn't write to me if I should ask him
to do so. I wish you would give me the
address of John's old sweetheart. She had
a book I should like so much to have.
One we used in school. Send it to
me if you can in your next letter
Did you get the red birds? answer!

Very Truly
Susan Anderson.

From S. Anderson M.D.
Fraser Colo.

W. H. Anderson.
2647 E. 14th Street
Oakland
California

Pa: It is so strange to me that I write you something I expect fully to hear from and wait and wait for an answer and wonder what has happened to keep you from writing. Then finally you write and wonder why you don't hear form me. I certainly do wish it could be possible for me to do something to take you out of the home where you are and care for you in a home of my own in some pleasant country. But it seems next to impossible. I certainly can not think of selling my home here & putting the proceeds into hunting for gold. It is too uncertain. This is the only shelter I have in the world and here is the only chance for income beside manual labor somewhere else and I am too old to go out to hand work for others. This month will make the end of 68 years for me. Too old to earn my keep by hand labor. I never did want to go to California to live, and nothing ever will make it attractive to me. Just now I don't care to go to the West coast on account of the possibility of war with Japan.

You will simply deride any thing I say in that direction so I might just as well not say it. I know how you think about California and no amount of argument will change you, but it doesn't appeal to me in any way whatever.

If I could get something in Indiana it would be home to me. I have met a lot of people from Missouri and Arkansas and think more of that country than California but it is not possible for me to get any thing. And as for selling my house you can't do it. There is no sale for any thing even good property in Denver will have to sell away down from the cost of building. It would be almost suicide for me to get rid of this. You can hunt gold without me giving up my only refuge. California was not such a pleasant place last Winter and this Winter isn't over yet. Yesterday was a stormy one here but not very cold. The wind blew & it snowed but not extremely low temperature. I am willing for you to hunt for gold if you don't put yourself in a helpless position as you did last time and then send for help to get out of the hole. I am not making any money but just living. What I made last summer must last me till Spring because there is no one here working now and it is almost impossible to collect back bills. Every body hangs on to money as hard as you ever saw. Just to have enough to eat on till Spring. There is no let up of hard times yet. Nothing in sight to make good times and a prospect of war.

Im sorry if Kenneth** is sick and there is no way I can help him because he wouldn't write to me if I should ask him to do so. I wish you would give me the address of John's old sweetheart. She has a book I should like so much to have. One we used in school. Send it to me if you can in your next letter. Did you get the red birds? Answer!

Very Truly
Susan Anderson.
** Kenneth was Doc's half-brother.

CHAPTER 08

WORLD WAR II

On December 7, 1941, Japanese bombed Pearl Harbor and the United States entered World War II. *Photo courtesy of Library of Congress, Prints and Photographs Division, LC-USW33-018433-C.*

Roger Richards was a World War II sailor who had received a very bad cut from a broken window while traveling through Colorado on the train. The train stopped in Fraser and Doc stitched up the wound. The two became good friends and kept in contact.

1941

Roger Richards' mother sent Doc two Hudson Bay blankets for taking such good care of her son. Doc also received a letter of commendation from the U.S. Navy for doing an outstanding job of treating Richards.

1944

Roger Richards was promoted to ensign. This is just one of many letters that Doc received from Navy sailors.

UNITED STATES NAVY

9 DECEMBER 1944

DEAR DR ANDERSON,

GREETING AND SALUTATIONS. I DON'T KNOW IF YOU HAVE HEARD FROM MY WIFE, CAROL, YET BUT SHE SAID SHE WOULD WRITE TO YOU.

WE WERE MARRIED AFTER AN EXTREMELY SHORT ROMANCE, A MATTER OF 8 DATES, BUT IT IS THE REAL THING FOR BOTH OF US. CAROL WAS A WAVE STOREKEEPER WHEN WE MET. SHE RECEIVED A MEDICAL DISCHARGE BUT WE LOST THE BABY AFTER ABOUT 5 WEEKS. MISCARRIAGE. WE WERE WAITING FOR SIX MONTHS TO GO BY BEFORE WE TRY AGAIN.

THERE IS NOT MUCH NEW TO WRITE ABOUT. THE SHIP IS A GOOD SHIP AND THE FOOD IS EXCELLENT. WE HAVE BEEN TRAVELLING ALL OVER THE PACIFIC AND NOW HAVE MORE THAN 40,000 MILES TO OUR CREDIT. IT IS A SMALL ESCORT CARRIER. KAISER BUILT IN VANCOUVER WASHINGTON. AND WELL BUILT FOR THE AMOUNT OF TIME IT TAKES TO PUT ONE OF THEM OUT.

I HEAR YOU ARE MOVING. DON'T FORGET TO LET US KNOW WHERE YOU LAND. AND WE WANT TO THANK YOU FOR THE PRESENT. I HAVE NOT SEEN IT YET BUT WILL DO SO AS SOON AS I GET BACK TO THE STATES NEXT TIME.

WELL THAT IS ABOUT ALL FOR NOW SO I'LL SAY MERRY XMAS AND A VERY HAPPY NEW YEAR TO YOU

REGARDS
ROGER RICHARDS

Drs. PACKARD and BARNARD
Orthopaedic Surgeons
1707 EAST 18th AVENUE
DENVER, COLORADO

February 18, 1942

Dr. Susan Anderson
Fraser
Colorado

Dear Doctor Anderson:

Mr. Price, whom you brought to St. Anthony's Hospital last night, expired this noon from shock and probable internal injuries. An autopsy has not been done yet, but I assume that the coroner will take charge of the body so I am unable to give definite diagnoses and definite cause of death.

Needless to say, in spite of all of our efforts--specifically, use of oxygen, intravenous glucose and plasma, coramine and strychnine--we were unable to overcome the shock he was in when you saw him last. He continued to go downhill from the time you saw him, and expired shortly after I had seen him the last time at 11:00 o'clock this morning.

Dr. Packard has asked me to report to you also that Mr. Kinney, with the eleven fractured ribs and pneumonia, died early this morning about 2:00 a. m., as we had anticipated. We are very sorry that both of these cases that you brought down had to expire but the types of injury were evidently altogether too much for them.

I trust that the weather in your country has abated some and it is much warmer at this time. With best regards, I am

Sincerely yours,

I. E. Hendrybon

IEH-m

1942

In addition to added work load, Doc continued to care for the Fraser community during WWII. This letter from February 18, 1942, is a colleague's report on two of Doc's patients she had referred to St. Anthony's Hospital in Denver.

During World War II, food, gasoline, and other necessities were rationed. To help the war effort, U. S. citizens were issued books of stamps (Ration Books) that allowed the purchase of a limited quantity of scarce items. This is one of Doc's Ration Books and instructions for use.

No. 102541AP

UNITED STATES OF AMERICA
OFFICE OF PRICE ADMINISTRATION

WAR RATION BOOK TWO

IDENTIFICATION

Susan Anderson
(Name of person to whom book is issued)

_____
(Street number or rural route)

Fraser   Cubo   72   F
(City or post office)   (State)   (Age) (Sex)

ISSUED BY LOCAL BOARD NO. 53   Grand
(County)

OFFICE
OF
PRICE ADM.

R-123

102541AP

Hot Sulphur Spr
(City)

_____
(Street address of local board)

By Leola M. Mossor
(Signature of issuing officer)

SIGNATURE _____
(To be signed by the person to whom this book is issued. If such person is unable to sign because of age or incapacity, another may sign in his behalf)

INSTRUCTIONS

1 This book is valuable. Do not lose it.

2 Each stamp authorizes you to purchase rationed goods in the quantities and at the times designated by the Office of Price Administration. Without the stamps you will be unable to purchase those goods.

3 Detailed instructions concerning the use of the book and the stamps will be issued from time to time. Watch for those instructions so that you will know how to use your book and stamps.

4 Do not tear out stamps except at the time of purchase and in the presence of the storekeeper, his employee, or a person authorized by him to make delivery.

5 Do not throw this book away when all of the stamps have been used, or when the time for their use has expired. You may be required to present this book when you apply for subsequent books.

Rationing is a vital part of your country's war effort. This book is your Government's guarantee of your fair share of goods made scarce by war, to which the stamps contained herein will be assigned as the need arises.

Any attempt to violate the rules is an effort to deny someone his share and will create hardship and discontent.

Such action, like treason, helps the enemy.

Give your whole support to rationing and thereby conserve our vital goods. Be guided by the rule:

"*If you don't need it,* **DON'T BUY IT.**"

U. S. GOVERNMENT PRINTING OFFICE: 1942   16—30853-1

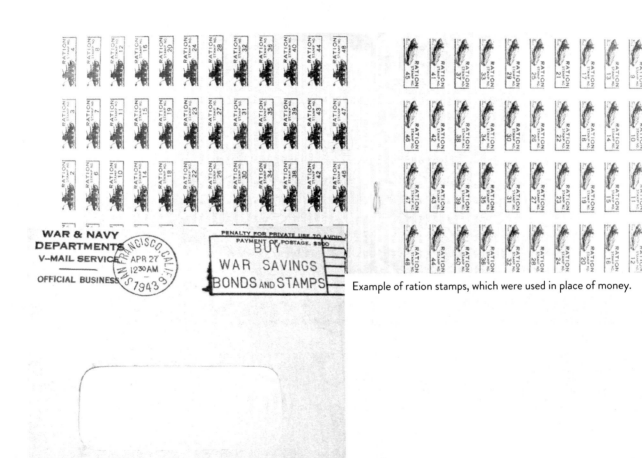

Example of ration stamps, which were used in place of money.

WWII Prisoners of War in Fraser

Photos of the camp and prisoners are used courtesy of Grand County Historical Association

German Prisoner of War Camp, Fraser, Colorado 1945-1946.

The United States built a prisoner of war camp in Fraser to house captured German soldiers. There were 200 German war prisoners assigned to the prison in Fraser. They worked for Morris Long and loaded an average of 25,000 feet of lumber on rail cars every day going to Grand Junction. They were paid 75 cents per day, which they could spend at the camp post exchange. Examples of their woodworking skills are on display at the Grand County Museum in Hot Sulphur Springs, Colorado. Doc treated both the American soldiers guarding the camp and the German prisoners.

According to the information posted at the Cozens Ranch Museum in Fraser, after the war the POW's wrote to Morris Long, who considered the prisoners family. The letters spoke about the good, understanding people who gave them opportunity to learn about the free country of the United States and expressed their gratitude.

Not all prisoners had a positive experience. Two prisoners in the camp committed suicide after learning that their families in German were all casualties of the war.

German prisoners in their work clothes.

The prisoners formed a band and played concerts for the town. They also played at Chuck Clayton's restaurant once a week.

For their hard work and good behavior, the prisoners were allowed to go to the local Fraser theater to watch movies.

Prisoners marching through Fraser. As they marched, they sang German songs. Townspeople lined both sides of the road to see and hear them.

Japan formally surrendered on September 2, 1945, thus ending World War II.

CHAPTER 09

DOC'S BRUSH WITH FAME

In 1943, PIC magazine came to Fraser to write a feature article about Doc. Photos in this chapter are from the article published in PIC, May 11, 1943.

Doc Susie, on the far left, visiting in the back of Carlson's General Store in Fraser.

Doc was a very strong lady. She often sawed and split her own wood. Sometimes a patient who could not afford to pay her for her services would help by splitting some wood for her.

Doc did not let the weather stop her from checking on patients during snowstorms.

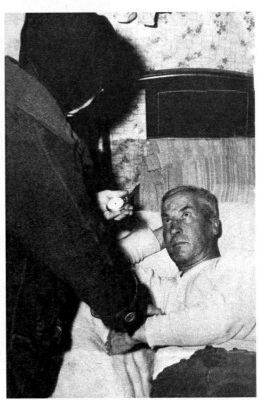

Doc Susie pleads with logger-blacksmith patient, Axel Bergstrom, 62, to go to a lower altitude, where he can recover from heart trouble.

Doc often used snowshoes or skis to get around when she called on patients in winter. When they were able, patients came to her office for treatment.

Doc examining a skier's sprained ankle at Winter Park ski area, which opened for its first season in 1940. Injured skiers added to Doc's workload.

Doc liked to embroider pillow cases and always incorporated roses into the designs. She liked roses the best and would cut out pictures of roses from seed catalogs and magazines and pin them to the walls of her office. Tatting was also one of her specialties.

Doc embroidering. Notice the cluttered desk in the background. Much of her house was cluttered in the same way.

Doc relaxing and perhaps thinking of times past. She had no pets after Pooch died and was by herself much of the time.

Also in 1943, actress Ethel Barrymore offered to make a movie of Doc's life story. She sent Doc roses and many letters asking her to consider the idea. "Fiddlesticks" was all Doc said about the possibility of a movie. Doc often expressed her disagreement by exclaiming "Fiddlesticks!" and "Fiddlesticks!" was her only comment on the movie idea. She was not interested. Many years later, when the television series "Dr. Quinn Medicine Woman" aired, many thought the main character was based on Doc Susie. There's no evidence that this was the case. Doc would have likely been displeased to have her life fictionalized on television.

The University of Michigan

HEREBY *it is certified that* **Susan Anderson** is a Member of

THE EMERITUS CLUB OF THE ALUMNI ASSOCIATION AL

and and is granted this Certificate in recognition of attendance at the Alumni Reunion

Anna marking the **50th** Anniversary of the graduation of **her** Class

Ann Arbor, June **14, 1947**

Doc, on far right, at the 50th reunion of her medical school class. *Courtesy of the Colorado Historical Society, 10025816.*

CHAPTER 10

DOC'S LAST YEARS IN FRASER

Aunt Hazel helped Doc apply for an old age pension by using a photograph from her 50th medical class reunion as proof of Doc's age. Doc was 77 years old in 1947. The town paid for Doc to attend the reunion.

In 1950, Uncle Bud found an abandoned fawn in the woods. He brought it home, and Aunt Hazel bottle fed and provided a safe place for it to live. Doc examined the fawn to make sure it was healthy before letting Aunt Hazel get too attached to it.

Aunt Hazel named it Doe-Doe because it was female. As Doe-Doe grew she became a nuisance to some of the town folks. Doc recommended giving her to the Denver Zoo, which Aunt Hazel did.

Whenever Uncle Bud and Aunt Hazel went to Denver, they always visited Doe-Doe at the zoo. Hazel would call Doe-Doe by name and Doe-Doe would run to her, and they always had a nice visit.

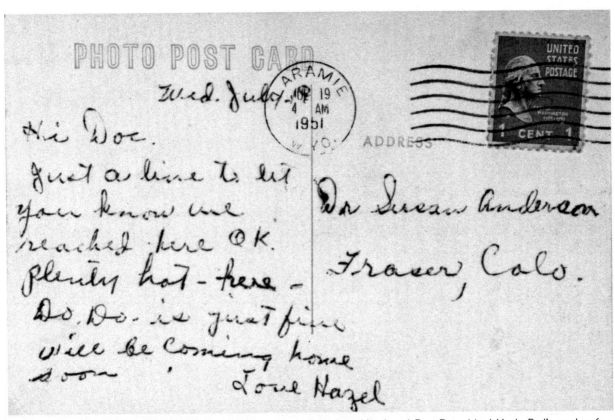

PHOTO POST CARD

Wed. July 19 1951

Hi Doc.
Just a line to let
you know we
reached here O.K.
Plenty hot - here -
Do. Do. is just fine
Will be coming home
soon
Love Hazel

ADDRESS

Dr Susan Anderson
Fraser, Colo.

A note to Doc assuring her that all had gone well when Uncle Bud, Aunt Hazel, and Doe-Doe visited Uncle Bud's mother (my grandmother) in Laramie, Wyoming, in 1951.

Doc would sometimes dress up and go to The Broadmoor Hotel in Colorado Springs for a well-earned vacation.

Sitting and thinking by the Fraser railroad depot in 1950.

Doc photographed in her yard on her way to Aunt Hazel's little house in the background.

ORIGINAL

TREASURER'S OFFICE, GRAND COUNTY, COLO.
No. 638

SCHEDULE 40

Hot Sulphur Springs, Colo., Feb. 9 1955

RECEIVED OF Susan Anderson

$ 16 64

ANDERSON, SUSAN
FRASER, COLORADO   SD 2

First Half
Second Half | payment of Taxes of **1954**
Full

on the following described property:

LOTS 34,35: BLK 2: EASTOM

DISTRIBUTION OF TAXES

State, County and Gen'l School Taxes	4 09	School Dist. No.	2	4 03
Moffat Tunnel Tax	44	" " "		
Metal Mining		" " "		
P. & L. Tax		" " "		
Predatory Animal Tax		" " "		
Special Grand Lake		" " "		
Grand Lake W. & S.		" " "		
Special Kremmling		" " "		
Kremmling Frontage		" " "		
Special Hot S. Springs		" " "		
H. S. S. Frontage		" " "		
Special Granby		" " "		
Granby Frontage		" " "		
Special Fraser	5 08	" " "		
Grand Fire P. Dist. No. 1		" " "		
Grand Fire P. Dist. No. 2		" " "		
M. P. Water Cons.	15	" " " 1 UH		
Granby Sanit. Dist.		" " " 2 UH		2 85
		" " " 1&2-2 UH		
		TAX TOTAL		16 64
Check—M.O.—Cash		Interest		
Amt. Rec'd.		Advertising		
Tax		Fees		
Change		TOTAL		16 64

Value of Real Estate - - - $ 290
Value of Personalty - - - $
Total Value of Property - $

Examine Your Receipt
and See That All Your
Property is Included.

Carl F. Fischer
County Treasurer
By _____ Deputy

The last tax receipt for her log home before Doc moved to the nursing home in Denver. The value of the real estate was $290. She paid $16.64 in taxes.

CHAPTER 11

DOC'S FINAL MOVE & RESTING PLACE

These houses at 1165 and 1175 Pennsylvania Street, Denver, were combined in 1930 to create the Samaritan Nursing Home. Doc lived there from 1956 until her death in 1960. At present, the complex is residential condominiums.

While Doc was a patient in the nursing home, Aunt Hazel and Aunt Minnie went to visit her one day. When they arrived at her private room, they noticed that she was all dressed up and sitting in her rocking chair. Aunt Hazel asked her why she was all dressed up. She said, "I am waiting for someone to pick me up and take me back to my home in Indiana. I am really going to enjoy all the roses."

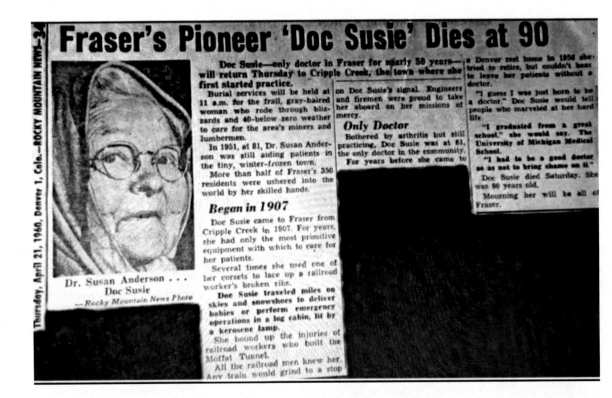

Fraser's Pioneer 'Doc Susie' Dies at 90

Dr. Susan Anderson . . . Doc Susie
—Rocky Mountain News Photo

Doc Susie—only doctor in Fraser for nearly 50 years—will return Thursday to Cripple Creek, the town where she first started practice.

Burial services will be held at 11 a.m. for the frail, gray-haired woman who rode through blizzards and 40-below zero weather to care for the area's miners and lumbermen.

In 1951, at 81, Dr. Susan Anderson was still aiding patients in the tiny, winter-frozen town.

More than half of Fraser's 350 residents were ushered into the world by her skilled hands.

Began in 1907

Doc Susie came to Fraser from Cripple Creek in 1907. For years, she had only the most primitive equipment with which to care for her patients.

Several times she used one of her corsets to lace up a railroad worker's broken ribs.

Doc Susie traveled miles on skies and snowshoes to deliver babies or perform emergency operations in a log cabin, lit by a kerosene lamp.

She bound up the injuries of railroad workers who built the Moffat Tunnel.

All the railroad men knew her. Any train would grind to a stop on Doc Susie's signal. Engineers and firemen were proud to take her aboard on her missions of mercy.

Only Doctor

Bothered by arthritis but still practicing, Doc Susie was at 81, the only doctor in the community.

For years before she came to

a Denver rest home in 1956 she tried to retire, but couldn't bear to leave her patients without a doctor.

"I guess I was just born to be a doctor," Doc Susie would tell people who marveled at her hard life.

"I graduated from a great school," she would say. The University of Michigan Medical School.

"I had to be a good doctor so as not to bring shame on it."

Doc Susie died Saturday. She was 90 years old.

Mourning her will be all of Fraser.

Doc's obituary from *The Rocky Mountain News*, April 21, 1960.

Doc Susie—only doctor in Fraser for nearly 50 years—will return Thursday to Cripple Creek, the town where she first started practice.

Burial services will be held at 11 a.m. for the frail, gray-haired woman who rode through blizzards and 40-below zero weather to care for the area's miners and lumbermen.

In 1951, at 81, Dr. Susan Anderson was still aiding patients in the tiny, winter-frozen town.

More than half of Fraser's 350 residents were ushered into the world by her skilled hands.

Began in 1907

Doc Susie cam to Fraser from Cripple Creek in 1907. For years, she had only the most primitive equipment with which to care for her patients.

Several times she used one of her corsets to lace up a railroad worker's broken ribs.

Doc Susie traveled miles on skies and snowshoes to deliver babies or perform emergency operations in a log cabin, lit by a kerosene lamp.

She bound up the injuries of railroad works who built the Moffat Tunnel.

All the railroad men knew her. Any train would grind to a stop on Doc Susie's signal. Engineers and firemen were proud to take her aboard on her missions of mercy.

Only Doctor

Bothered by arthritis but still practicing, Doc Susie was at 81, the only doctor in the community.

For years before she came to a Denver rest home in 1956, she tried to retire but couldn't bear to leave her patients without a doctor.

"I guess I was just born to be a doctor," Doc Susie would tell people who marveled at her hard life.

"I graduated from a great school," she would say. The University of Michigan Medical School.

"I had to be a good doctor so as not to bring shame on it."

Doc Susie died Saturday. She was 90 years old. Mourning her will be all of Fraser.

It was Doc's wish that she be buried in the Mt. Pisgah Cemetery in Cripple Creek where her brother John had been laid to rest in 1900.

CHAPEL of the CHIMES
1331 Sherman

CHAPEL of the ANGELS
7177 W. Colfax   TA 5-0151

ANDERSON—

Dr. Susan Anderson, 1165 Pennsylvania, formerly of Fraser, Colo. Sister of Cuba Brady, Marine City, Mich., Mrs. Stephen Dam, Columbus, Ohio, Cozette Anderson, San Jose, Calif. Services our CHAPEL OF THE CHIMES, 1331 SHERMAN, today, 1 p.m. Interment Cripple Creek, Colo.

The announcement of the time and place of Doc's funeral.

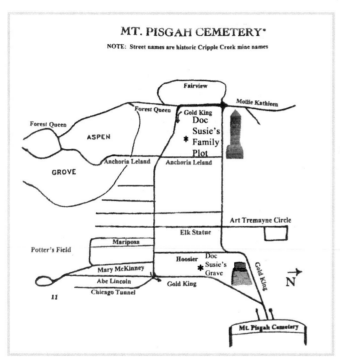

MT. PISGAH CEMETERY*

NOTE: Street names are historic Cripple Creek mine names

Fairview

Mollie Kathleen

Forest Queen

Gold King

Forest Queen

Doc Susie's Family Plot

ASPEN

Anchoria Leland

Anchoria Leland

GROVE

Art Tremayne Circle

Elk Statue

Mariposa

Potter's Field

Hoosier

Doc Susie's Grave

Mary McKinney

Gold King

Abe Lincoln

Gold King

Chicago Tunnel

11

N

Mt. Pisgah Cemetery

A map of Mt. Pisgah Cemetery in Cripple Creek showing location of Doc's family plot and the actual location of her grave. *Map courtesy of the City of Cripple Creek and the Mt. Pisgah Cemetery Board of Directors.*

Doc is not buried in the family plot, although that was her wish. When the time came, the burial crew was unable to find the family plot due to the large amount of snow covering the cemetery.

In 1992, Doc Susie's biographer, Virginia Cornell, paid for the inscription on the Anderson family plot marker. The inscription reads:

Susan Anderson M.D.
Died April 16, 1960
AGED
90Y 2M 16D
Doctor of Grand County

Doc Susie is actually buried in this gravesite in the Pisgah Cemetery in Cripple Creek. The headstone was donated by the townspeople of Fraser after they learned that Doc's grave was unmarked.

Doc Susie's license to practice medicine in Colorado.

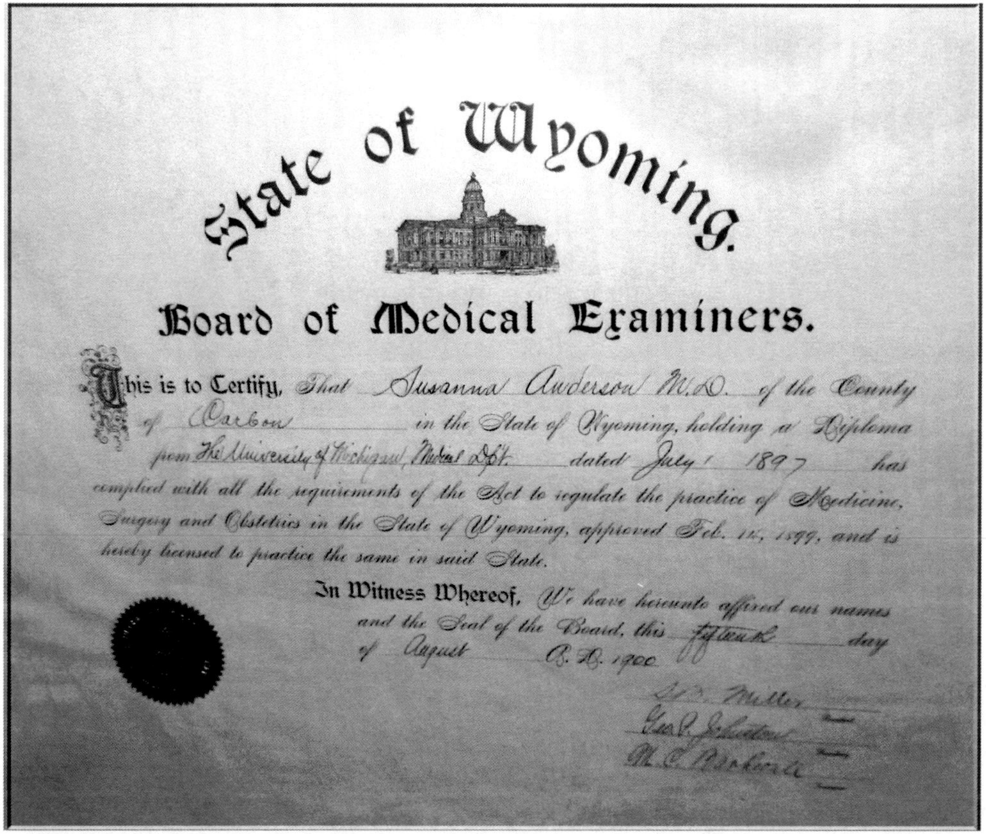

State of Wyoming.

Board of Medical Examiners.

This is to Certify, That Susanna Anderson M.D. of the County of Carbon in the State of Wyoming, holding a Diploma from The University of Michigan, Medical Dept. dated July 1 1897 has complied with all the requirements of the Act to regulate the practice of Medicine, Surgery and Obstetrics in the State of Wyoming, approved Feb. 16, 1899, and is hereby licensed to practice the same in said State.

In Witness Whereof, We have hereunto affixed our names and the Seal of the Board, this fifteenth day of August A.D. 1900

[illegible]

Doc's license to practice medicine in the state of Wyoming.

AMERICAN ASSOCIATION OF

RAILWAY  SURGEONS

FOR THE PROMOTION AND IMPROVEMENT OF RAILWAY
SURGERY BY THE INTERCHANGE OF IDEAS AND THE
CULTIVATION OF ACQUAINTANCE AND FRATERNAL RELATIONS
AMONG THOSE ACTIVELY ENGAGED IN THIS SPECIAL WORK
HAS ELECTED

SUSAN ANDERSON

ACTIVE MEMBER

James E W Thomson
PRESIDENT

DB Kepner MD
SECRETARY

NOVEMBER 8, 1948

Doc served as a railroad doctor (or railway surgeon) for a number of years.

The Colorado
State Board of Medical Examiners

No. 417

THIS IS TO CERTIFY THAT Susan Anderson M. D.

Address Fraser, Colorado

Has paid the Annual Registration Fee for the year designated hereon and is thereby entitled to practice MEDICINE until December 31 of same year under the license issued to him/her by this Board.

This certificate shall at all times be conspicuously displayed in your office.

1930

Colorado State Board of Medical Examiners

Registration No. 740

Receipt No. P-783

License No. -2590-

Issued Jan. 15, 1946

Fee $ 2.00

1946

This is to Certify that,

SUSAN ANDERSON, M.D.
Fraser
Colorado

to whom the above numbered license to practice

MEDICINE

was issued, has complied with the law governing the Annual Registration of such licenses and is hereby entitled to practice medicine in the State of Colorado during the year ending December 31, 1946.

This certificate must be displayed in your office at all times.

EXPIRES DECEMBER 31, 1946

The Colorado
State Board of Medical Examiners

No. 417

THIS IS TO CERTIFY THAT Susan Anderson, M. D.

Address Fraser, Colorado

Has paid the Annual Registration Fee for the year designated hereon and is thereby entitled to practice MEDICINE until December 31 of same year under the license issued to him/her by this Board.

This certificate shall at all times be conspicuously displayed in your office.

1931

Colorado State Board of Medical Examiners

Registration No. 1469

Receipt No. Q-1516

License No. - 2590 -

Issued Jan. 8, 1947

Fee $ 2.00

1947

This is to Certify that,

SUSAN ANDERSON, M.D.
Fraser
Colorado

to whom the above numbered license to practice

MEDICINE

was issued, has complied with the law governing the Annual Registration of such licenses and is hereby entitled to practice medicine in the State of Colorado during the year ending December 31, 1947.

This certificate must be displayed in your office at all times.

EXPIRES DECEMBER 31, 1947

Some of the certificates that had to renewed annually in order for Doc to practice medicine in Colorado.

Appendix B

REPRESENTATIVE MEDICAL PRESCRIPTIONS

A prescription from 1910 included quinine and phenyl salicylate.

This 1908 prescription included Ichthyol, Belladonna, and Glycerin for a patient.

Although she very seldom administered or prescribed narcotics, as a responsible physician she made sure she had a supply of pain killers and the special permits required to use them.

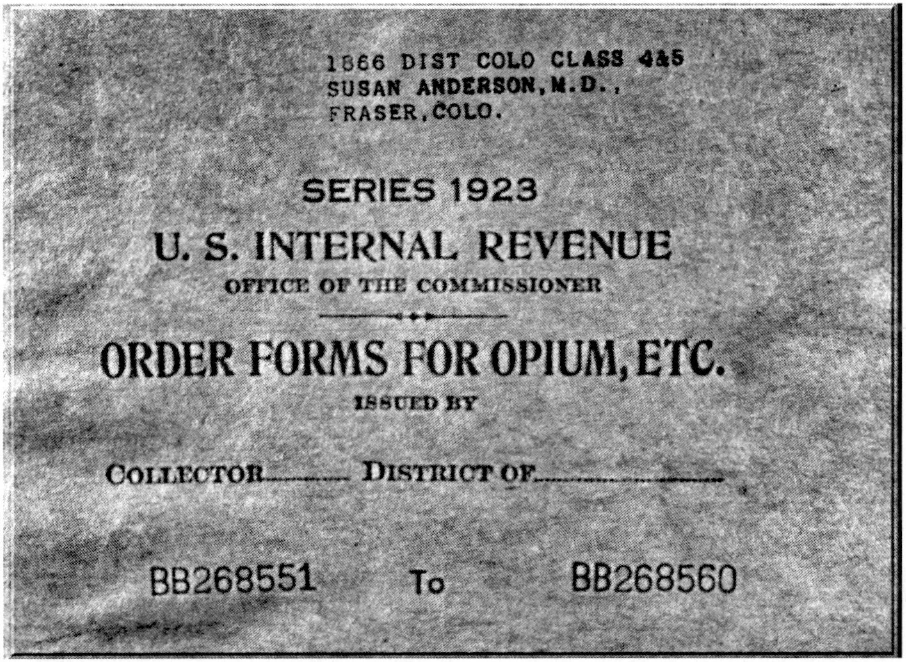

1866 DIST COLO CLASS 4&5
SUSAN ANDERSON, M.D.,
FRASER, COLO.

SERIES 1923

U. S. INTERNAL REVENUE

OFFICE OF THE COMMISSIONER

ORDER FORMS FOR OPIUM, ETC.

ISSUED BY

COLLECTOR_____ DISTRICT OF_____

BB268551   To   BB268560

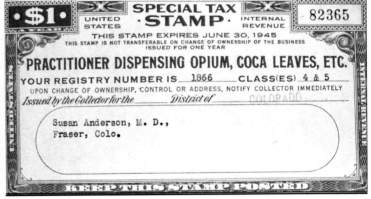

TREASURY DEPARTMENT
DUPLICATE

UNITED STATES INTERNAL REVENUE ORDER FORM FOR OPIUM
OR COCA LEAVES, OR COMPOUNDS, MANUFACTURES, SALTS,
DERIVATIVES OR PREPARATIONS THEREOF UNDER SECTION 2
OF THE ACT OF CONGRESS, APPROVED DECEMBER 17, 1914.

SERIES OF 1923

Special tax under said Act in each of the classes and at the location specified below must be paid for a fiscal period covering the date inserted by the purchaser before this form may be used.

No. BB268551   DATE Sept 22 1924   THIS ORDER IS FOR EXACTLY 2 ITEMS.

1866 DIST COLO CLASS 4&5
SUSAN ANDERSON, M.D.,
FRASER, COLO.

ISSUED DEC 29 1923 BY F. W. HOWBERT

To
STREET   CITY   STATE

TO BE FILLED IN BY PURCHASER

ITEM	CATALOGUE NUMBER	NUMBER OF PACKAGES	SIZE OF PACKAGE	NAME OF ARTICLE	NUMBER OF STAMPED PACKAGES FURNISHED	DATE FILLED
1		1	20 Tablets	Morph. Sulph. ½ gr.		
2		1	20 Tab.	Cocain HCl 1/100 gr.		
3			P			
4			L			
5			I			
6			C			
7			A			
8			T			
9			E			
10						

Susan Anderson, M.D.
SIGNATURE OF PURCHASER

$1

SPECIAL TAX STAMP

UNITED STATES   INTERNAL REVENUE

82365

THIS STAMP EXPIRES JUNE 30, 1945
THIS STAMP IS NOT TRANSFERABLE ON CHANGE OF OWNERSHIP OF THE BUSINESS
ISSUED FOR ONE YEAR

PRACTITIONER DISPENSING OPIUM, COCA LEAVES, ETC.

YOUR REGISTRY NUMBER IS 1866   CLASS(ES) 4 & 5

UPON CHANGE OF OWNERSHIP, CONTROL OR ADDRESS, NOTIFY COLLECTOR IMMEDIATELY

Issued by the Collector for the   District of   COLORADO

Susan Anderson, M. D.,
Fraser, Colo.

KEEP THIS STAMP POSTED

Appendix C
INVOICES AND MEDICAL ADVERTISEMENTS

Doc's $40 invoice for 'Care in Influenza'.

Doc used this statement of accounts to bill patients. The notes at the bottom of the page include this reminder: "The modern doctor needs a great deal of money other than his actual living expenses. He must have transportation facilities to go anywhere at any time. He must have apparatus, books, drugs and instruments to maintain an efficiency of the highest degree. His patients must help him maintain that efficiency."

STATEMENT

FRASER, COLO......................................192....

M..

IN ACCOUNT WITH

SUSAN ANDERSON, M. D.

TO PROFESSIONAL SERVICES RENDERED FROM........................TO......

MEDICAL	.	$......................
SURGICAL	.	$......................
OBSTETRICAL	.	$......................

CREDITS $......................

BALANCE DUE $......................

RECEIVED PAYMENT..

THE ABOVE IS A STATEMENT OF YOUR ACCOUNT. IF INCORRECT, PLEASE RETURN

TO BE A BUSINESS SUCCESS A DOCTOR MUST COLLECT HIS ACCOUNTS EVERY THIRTY DAYS.

The courtesy of thirty days' time is extended to all with approved credit.

By getting a statement every thirty days and checking it with your memorandum, misunderstandings are avoided.

The modern doctor needs a great deal of money other than his actual living expenses. He must have transportation facilities to go anywhere at any time. He must have apparatus, books, drugs and instruments to maintain an efficiency of the highest degree. His patients must help him maintain that efficiency.

The doctor does not like to be rated "poor pay" any more than you do. Unless he collects his money he cannot pay his bills.

There is no legitimate reason for keeping your doctor waiting for his money any more than you do your grocer or your butcher. His ability to serve must, in a measure, be governed by his collections for past services.

If Not Convenient to Make Immediate Payment, Partial Payment or Settlement by Bankable Notes Will Be Appreciated.

Copyrighted in 1923 by A. F. Armstrong.

PHARMACEUTICAL ADVERTISEMENTS

TEN COMMANDMENTS
for High Blood Pressure Sufferers

1. Thou shalt honour thy doctor's commands and obey them.
2. Thou shalt not eat nor drink to excess.
3. Thou shalt take life easy and live longer.
4. Thou shalt sleep eight hours every night.
5. Thou shalt rest one hour after the noon meal.
6. Thou shalt not lose thy temper for any reason.
7. Thou shalt not brood nor worry over spilt milk.
8. Thou shalt not covet thy neighbor's wealth but work less.
9. Thou shalt not covet thy neighbor's dinner but eat less.
10. Thou shalt take thy doctor's prescription and nothing else.

Doctor: If you wish to give these "Ten Commandments" to a patient, please detach same from this portion of card. If you want more of these cards, just let us know quantity and we will be glad to supply same to you.

Allimin
Concentrated Garlic-Parsley Tablets

For reduction of blood-pressure and relief of associated headache and dizziness in essential hypertension. Average dose: 2 tablets after meals t.i.d., omitting the fourth day.

VAN PATTEN PHARMACEUTICAL CO.
54 W. Illinois St.   Chicago

WE AIM TO GIVE THE BEST GOODS AND BEST SERVICE

T. T. BEATTIE
DISPENSING CHEMIST AND OPTICIAN

PHONE QUEEN 506   462 BRONSON AVE., COR. GLADSTONE OTTAWA

IF YOU ARE NOT SATISFIED WITH GOODS OR TREATMENT, TELL US. IF YOU ARE, TELL OTHERS.

Appendix D
DOC SUSIE'S PERSONAL ITEMS

Aunt Hazel was the executor of Doc's estate. She had the monumental task of deciding what to do with the things in Doc's house.

Doc's nephew, Roger Brady, selected the few items he wanted. Aunt Hazel gave some items to the museums in Hot Sulphur Springs, Fraser, and Cripple Creek.

It was reported that Doc had a habit of hiding money in her books and magazines, so all those items were searched.

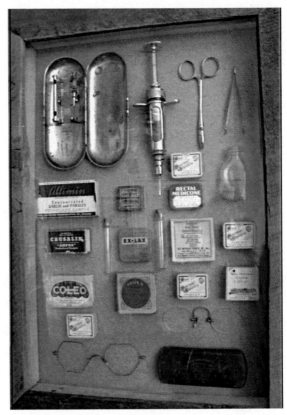

I arranged these items used by Doc and framed them with wood from Uncle Bud's barn.

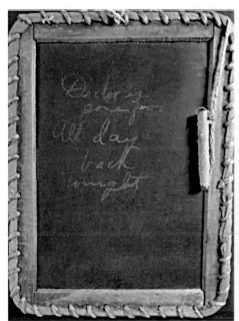

Signs used by Doc let her patients know when she was out of her office and the homes that were quarantined due to whopping cough.

Doc's best dresses.

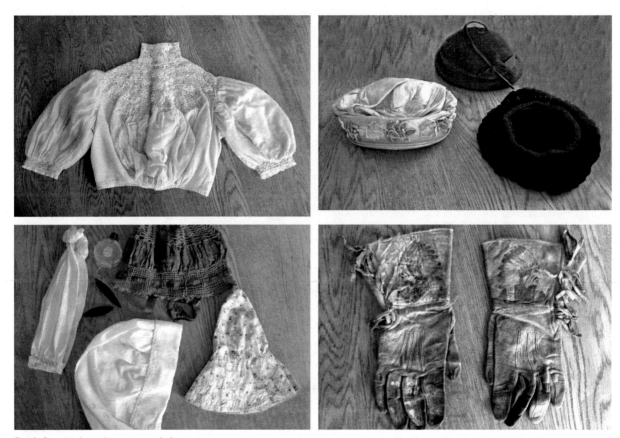

Doc's favorite hats, bonnets, and gloves.

Doc carried a 'miser's bag' to hold money and small items. They were crocheted or knitted by hand.

Doc owned fancier purses for special occasions, such as her times of rest at The Broadmoor Hotel.

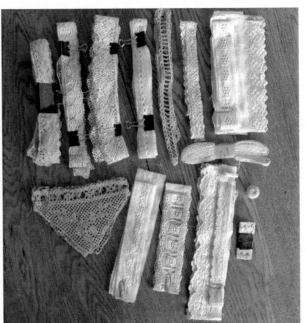

Doc's sewing items.

Some of Doc's shoes.

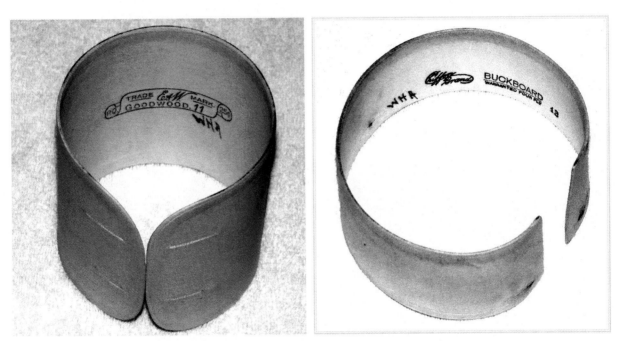

Shirt collars owned by Doc's father. Note the initials, WHA, penned inside the collars.

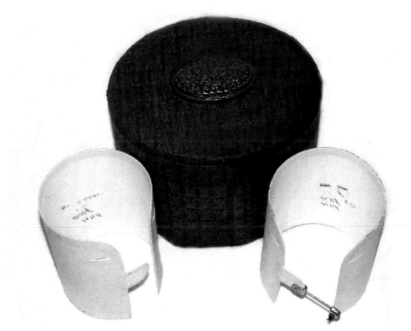

Shirt Cuffs | In the 1908 Sears and Roebuck Catalog, shirt cuffs were priced at 7 cents each.

Appendix F
WILLS OF WILLIAM H. ANDERSON & SUSAN ANDERSON

LAST WILL AND TESTAMENT

I, William H. Andwerson, of the City of Denver, Colorado, being of sound mind and disposing memory, do hereby make, declare and publish this my Last Will and Testament, hereby revoking any and all wills heretofore by me made.

I direct that all my just debts be first paid out of my estate.

To each of my children Cozette (duaghter), Vernon (son) and Kenneth (son), I give and bequeath the sum of ONE Dollar;

All the remainder of my estate, real, personal and mixed, and wherever situate, I give and bequeath in fee simple absolute to my daughter Susan Anderson of the Town of Frazer, Colorado.

I hereby name my daughter Susan Anderson of Frazer Colorado, as the executrix of this last will and testament, and I request that she be allowed to serve as such executrix without bond.

Done at Denver, State of Colorado, this 1st day of April 1925.

William H. Anderson

We the undersigned witnesses to the above and foregoing last will and testament of William H. Anderson, do hereby declare that William H. Anderson declared to us that the foregoing is his last will and testament, that we signed the same as witnesses thereto at his request and in his presence and in the presence of each other, and that said William H. Anderson signed the same in the presence of each of us, this 1st day of April A. D. 1925 at Denver, Colorado.

Alexander Nenne
Foris Wagner

LAST WILL AND TESTAMENT OF
SUSAN ANDERSON

IN THE NAME OF GOD, AMEN: I, SUSAN ANDERSON of Fraser, Grand County, Colorado, being of sound and disposing mind and memory do make, publish and declare this to be my last will and testament, hereby revoking any and all other and former wills or codicils by me at any time heretofore made.

I.

I direct that all of my just debts, including expenses of last illness expenses and expenses of administration of my estate, be by my executor, hereinafter named paid as soon as may be after my death.

II.

I give, devise and bequeath all of the rest residue and remainder of my estate, real, personal or mixed and wheresoever situated to my nephew, Roger Brady of Marine City, Michigan.

III

I hereby nominate and appoint M. L. Fesler of Fraser, Grand County, Colorado, to be the executor of this my last will and testament and direct that he be permitted by the Count to serve without surety on his bond, and since he has expressed his intention of not accepting any compensation for his services in such capacity, I hereby direct that he be permitted to select such item or items of my personal belongings as he may desire as his own property.

IV.

It is my desire that my body be burried in the Anderson Plot in the Mt. Misgah Cemetary in Cripple Creek, Colorado.

IN WITNESS WHEREOF I have hereunto set my hand and seal this 23rd day of June, A. D. 1954.

Copy

/s/ Susan Anderson (SEAL)

2.

ATTESTATION

The above and foregoing instrument, consisting of this and one preceeding page, identified by the signature of the Testatrix was by her, signed, sealed, published and declared as and for her Last Will and Testament, in our presence and in the presence of each of us, and we at her request, in her presence and in the presence of each other, subscribed our names as attesting witnesses thereto this 23rd day of June, A. D. 1954

/s/ Ona Fesler   of   Fraser, Colorado

/s/ Hugh Gilmore   of Hot Sulphur Springs, Colo.

Copy

It is understood that M. H. Fesler was not available to perform the duties of Executor as directed in this will. Consequently, Hazel Briggs was chosen to perform those duties as directed by Doctor Susan Anderson.

Appendix G
REMEMBERING DOC TODAY

Cozens Ranch Museum in Fraser, Colorado. Upstairs, one room is dedicated to Doc Susie. *Photos courtesy of Grand County Historical Association.*

Author Owen Briggs with items donated by his Aunt Hazel Briggs on display at Cozens Ranch Museum.

Doc's operating table was donated to the Cozens Ranch Museum by Hazel Briggs.

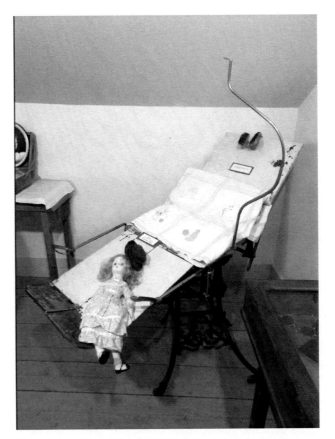

Photo courtesy of Grand County Historical Association.

Photos courtesy of Grand County Historical Association.

The Cozens Ranch Museum also displays the Bible Doc Susie carried on her rounds. A feather she used to mark her place in the Old Testament, her medical bag, her snowshoes, her surgical instruments, and her pistols are displayed on the following pages. Doc always carried a pistol to scare away robbers and mountain lions.

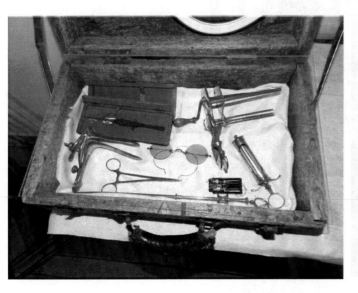

A quilt depicting Doc was created by Carol Kitts and donated to Grand County Historical Association.

Grand County Pioneer Village Museum in Hot Sulphur Springs, Colorado, has numerous items on display that belonged to Doc Susie. One item is the baby scale from her medical office.

The Museum in Cripple Creek, Colorado, displays some items related to Doc's life in the mining town.

One of the main streets in Fraser is named for Doc Susie.

Originally sculpted in wood by Jim Hoy, the bronze sculpture is part of The Walk through History Park in Fraser. About a bronze statue of her likeness, it's easy to imagine Doc Susie saying, "Fiddlesticks!"

Photo courtesy of Jim Hoy.

Black, Robert C., III. *Island in the Rockies.* Grand County Pioneer Society. Boulder, Colorado: Pruett Publishing Co., 1969.

Bollinger, Edward T. *Rails that Climb: A Narrative History of the Moffat Road.* Golden, Colorado: Colorado Railroad Museum, 1979.

Cornell, Virginia. *Doc Susie: The True Story of a Country Physician in the Colorado Rockies.* Tucson, Arizona: Manifest Publications, 1991.

Cunningham, Penny. *Doc Susie: Mountain Doctor.* Palmer Lake, Colorado: Filter Press, 2010.

Enss, Chris. *The Doctor Wore Petticoats.* Billings, Montana: Two Dot, 2006.

Griffin, Lydia. *Susan Anderson: Colorado's Doc Susie.* Palmer Lake, Colorado: Filter Press, 2010.

Robertson, Janet. *The Magnificent Mountain Women.* Lincoln, NE: Bison Books, 2003.

FURTHER READING

ABOUT THE AUTHOR

Owen Manfred Briggs was born in Denver, Colorado. When he was five years old, he and his two sisters were taken from their parents by the Social Services because his father was an alcoholic and abusive.

After his parents divorced, his mother's second husband refused to let her children live with them. His sisters were placed in Denver Orphans' Home, and he went to live with his Uncle Bud (Basil Kennedy) Briggs and Aunt Hazel in Fraser, Colorado. Doc Susie lived next door to the Briggs. She was 69 years old when Owen met her.

After four years with Uncle Bud, Owen lived for six months with his father before Social Services again intervened. He lived in five foster homes then returned to his Uncle Bud and Aunt Hazel's home. He graduated from Middle Park High School in Granby before joining the Navy in 1953 where he served for 23 years. He worked for the U.S. Postal Service for ten years before retiring. Owen and Dorie Briggs live in Colorado Springs, Colorado.